access to

943.03

LUTHER *and the* GERMAN REFORMATION 1517–55

Second Edition

Keith Randell

Hodder Murray

A MEMBER OF THE HODDER HEADLINE GROUP

Acknowledgements
The front cover illustration shows Martin Luther by Lucas Cranach, the
elder (1477-1553) reproduced courtesy of Kurpfalzisches, Germany/
Giraudon/Bridgeman Art Library.

The publishers would like to thank the following for permission to
reproduce copyright illustrations in this book:

Bildarchiv PreussischerKulturbesitz, pages 46 & 69; Hulton Getty, page 33;
Katz Pictures Ltd/Mansell/Time Inc, page 26

Every effort has been made to trace and acknowledge ownership of
copyright. The publishers will be glad to make suitable arrangements with
any copyright holders whom it has not been possible to contact.

Orders: please contact Bookpoint Ltd, 130 Milton Park, Abingdon,
Oxon OX14 4SB. Telephone: (44) 01235 827720 Fax: (44) 01235 400454.
Lines are open from 9 am – 6 pm, Monday to Saturday, with a 24 hour
message answering service. You can also order through our website:
www.hoddereducation.co.uk

British Library Cataloguing in Publication Data

A catalogue record for this title is available from the British Library

ISBN-10: 0 340 74929 6
ISBN-13: 978 0 340 749296

First published 2000

Impression number   10 9   8   7   6
Year   2005

The cover illustration shows a portrait of Luther by Lucas Cranach, reproduced
courtesy of Photographie Giraudon.

Typeset by Sempringham publishing services, Bedford.
Printed in Great Britain for Hodder Murray, an imprint of Hodder Education,
a member of the Hodder Headline Group, 338 Euston Road, London NW1 3BH
by CPI Bath

Contents

Preface

To the general reader

Although the *Access to History* series has been designed with the needs of students studying the subject at higher examination levels very much in mind, it also has a great deal to offer the general reader. The main body of the text (i.e. ignoring the 'Study Guides' at the ends of chapters) forms a readable and yet stimulating survey of a coherent topic as studied by historians. However, each author's aim has not merely been to provide a clear explanation of what happened in the past (to interest and inform): it has also been assumed that most readers wish to be stimulated into thinking further about the topic and to form opinions of their own about the significance of the events that are described and discussed (to be challenged). Thus, although no prior knowledge of the topic is expected on the reader's part, she or he is treated as an intelligent and thinking person throughout. The author tends to share ideas and possibilities with the reader, rather than passing on numbers of so-called 'historical truths'.

To the student reader

Although advantage has been taken of the publication of a second edition to ensure the results of recent research are reflected in the text, the main alteration from the first edition is the inclusion of new features, and the modification of existing ones, aimed at assisting you in your study of the topic at AS level, A level and Higher. Two features are designed to assist you during your first reading of a chapter. The *'Points to Consider'* section following each chapter title is intended to focus your attention on the main theme(s) of the chapter, and the issues box following most section headings alerts you to the question or questions to be dealt with in the section. The *'Working on ...'* section at the end of each chapter suggests ways of gaining maximum benefit from the chapter.

There are many ways in which the series can be used by students studying History at a higher level. It will, therefore, be worthwhile thinking about your own study strategy before you start your work on this book. Obviously, your strategy will vary depending on the aim you have in mind, and the time for study that is available to you.

If, for example, you want to acquire a general overview of the topic in the shortest possible time, the following approach will probably be the most effective:

1. Read Chapter 1. As you do so, keep in mind the issues raised in the *'Points to Consider'* section.
2. Read the *'Points to Consider'* section at the beginning of Chapter 2 and decide whether it is necessary for you to read this chapter.

3. If it is, read the chapter, stopping at each heading or sub-heading to note down the main points that have been made. Often, the best way of doing this is to answer the question(s) posed in the Issues boxes.

4. Repeat stage 2 (and stage 3 where appropriate) for all the other chapters.

If, however, your aim is to gain a thorough grasp of the topic, taking however much time is necessary to do so, you may benefit from carrying out the same procedure with each chapter, as follows:

1. Read the chapter as fast as you can, and preferably at one sitting. As you do this, bear in mind any advice given in the *'Points to Consider'* section.

2. Study the flow diagram at the end of the chapter, ensuring that you understand the general 'shape' of what you have just read.

3. Read the *'Working on ...'* section and decide what further work you need to do on the chapter. In particularly important sections of the book, this is likely to involve reading the chapter a second time and stopping at each heading and sub-heading to think about (and probably to write a summary of) what you have just read.

4. Attempt the *'Source-based questions'* section. It will sometimes be sufficient to think through your answers, but additional understanding will often be gained by forcing yourself to write them down.

When you have finished the main chapters of the book, study the 'Further Reading' section and decide what additional reading (if any) you will do on the topic.

This book has been designed to help make your studies both enjoyable and successful. If you can think of ways in which this could have been done more effectively, please contact us. In the meantime, we hope that you will gain greatly from your study of History.

Keith Randell

1 The Background to the Reformation

POINTS TO CONSIDER

1. The Reformation is not an event in the way that, for example, a battle or an act of parliament is. It is the name thought up by historians to describe a series of happenings that seemed to them to be linked. Because they are dealing with an historical concept not with something that actually happened different historians have chosen to define the Reformation in different ways, making their own assumptions and bringing their own prejudices. It is important for you to be aware of what these are and of the dangers attached to them. A major implication of this is that you need to be aware of which definition is being used by any writer whose work on the Reformation you read. As you make your way through the first two sections of this chapter try to identify which assumptions the term 'the Reformation' carries with it and what definition of the term is going to be used throughout this book.

2. Historians spend most of their time researching and writing about *what* happened in the past. But what tends to excite them most is speculating about *why* the events they are describing took place - what their causes were. This is because there is rarely any certainty about causes (the evidence is always very partial and open to differing interpretations) which allows each writer to put forward an interpretation which seems convincing to him or her. The discussion of causes is also thought to be important because little sense can be made of events unless there is some understanding of why they happened. This is why the second half of this chapter focuses on a discussion of the causes of the Reformation. You need to develop some understanding of this topic so that the remainder of the book will make as much sense to you as possible. As you read section 3 for the first time make a mental note of the main issues historians have considered to be important in any discussion of the causes of the Reformation.

1 Introduction

> **KEY ISSUE** What questionable assumptions lie behind the way in which the Reformation has traditionally been studied?

a) Traps to Avoid

The Reformation has been studied by more historians than almost any other topic. It has been a source of fascination for tens of thousands of students over several centuries, and there is no sign of the interest abating. It is controversial in the extreme. There are very few aspects of it over which there is general agreement. Even some matters of factual detail are hotly disputed. In most years there are at least ten new books, based on original research, published on the subject. Therefore the pace at which additional evidence becomes available is somewhat bewildering and the general picture rarely becomes clearer in the process. Each new piece of research tends to throw into doubt at least some of the simple generalisations that have long been current on the subject. On this topic, more than most others, it is essential for the student to appreciate the provisional nature of our understanding and to accept that today's truth might be tomorrow's misinterpretation. I suspect that it is this very element of uncertainty that attracts so many people to the study of the Reformation.

Of course, it must be remembered that 'the Reformation' is a concept invented by historians, and used to describe the sequence of events by which large numbers of the inhabitants of Germany, Switzerland, Scandinavia, the Netherlands and Great Britain turned their backs on Catholicism and became members of independent Protestant churches. 'The Reformation' was not a term used at the time, or for several generations afterwards. It was popularised in the eighteenth century by Protestant historians in Germany who assumed unquestioningly that 'the Reformation' had been a process by which large numbers of ardent Christians, unable to accept the widespread abuses of the Catholic Church, had broken away to form their own purified religion. The very word 'Reformation' implies that the changes were for the better and were putting right what was wrong. In fact, the way in which the concept has been central to our study of sixteenth-century European history for more than 200 years has been a great propaganda victory for Protestantism. It is now far too late to attempt to abandon the concept, or even to change its name - several centuries of calling it 'the Desertion' might correct the balance - but we must at least try to be aware that when we accept the idea of 'the Reformation' as a framework for historical study, we are in danger of swallowing a considerable number of questionable assumptions and value judgements at the same time.

If this is true of the Reformation as a whole, it is particularly true of the Reformation in Germany, where the followers of Martin Luther have tended to dominate the study of the subject and have conditioned many people into an unthinking acceptance that Luther and Lutheranism are synonymous with the Reformation. A whole mythology has grown up around his life and it is now very difficult to disentangle fact from fiction. This has led numbers of historians to suggest that we would be more likely to arrive at a proper understanding of what happened during the Reformation in Germany if we were to take Luther from the centre of the stage and replace him with the 'ordinary man', focusing not on the leader but on the led. This, it is argued, would allow us to formulate meaningful answers to questions such as: 'Why did the Reformation take place where and when it did?', 'Why did it spread so widely and so rapidly?', and 'What effect did it have on the lives of the people?'

However, a student approaching the topic for the first time will need to become acquainted with the Luther-centred approach to begin with. Without that it is very difficult to make any sense of the welter of conflicting interpretations that surround the more wide-ranging approaches to the subject. But it is vital to remember at all times that Luther was not exclusively important. There is evidence that he was massively influential, but that is very different from claiming that other people and other factors did not also have a major effect on what happened.

Just as it is necessary, when following a Luther-centred approach, to remind oneself constantly of the danger of slipping unnoticed into typical Protestant assumptions about what happened in the Reformation, so it is important to realise that the choice of the start and end dates of 1517 and 1555 for the German Reformation can hide other equally dangerous assumptions. The most serious of these is that made by historians of the so-called Whig school (named after the British political party of the eighteenth and nineteenth centuries which shared the same general assumptions). The Whig historians, who were at their most influential a century ago, judged the importance of an event by its eventual consequences. They believed in the 'march of progress'. In their view, history was important because it explained how the present came to be as it is. They were, therefore, not very interested in trying to gauge the significance that events had at the time of their happening: they preferred to concentrate on the part they played in the long chain of causes and effects that leads from the past to the present.

b) Date Conventions

So, because Luther was of central importance to the movement, it was automatically assumed that the start date for the Reformation in Germany should be when he first publicly protested about what he regarded as shortcomings in the Church. This implies that, once Luther had made his initial protest, the Reformation was certain to follow. But the temptation to use historical hindsight is to be resisted, and it must be remembered that not until the late 1520s did it seem inevitable that the unity of the Church would be permanently shattered. So 1517 is used here as a convenient start date only because it is both traditional and as convenient (or inconvenient) as any other, and not because it is viewed as signalling the beginning of the Reformation in any clear-cut sense. A general movement such as the Reformation (or the Industrial Revolution) cannot meaningfully be said to have started on a specific date.

The same, of course, can be said of the end date for the Reformation in Germany. The tradition of fixing this at 1555 was established by Lutheran writers and has been followed by most others. But this date only has validity if one makes some huge assumptions. The Peace of Augsburg took place in 1555. This involved the rulers of the more than 300 virtually independent states and territories of Germany agreeing that each prince and city government should be free to choose between two religions - Catholicism and Lutheranism - and that everybody living within that territory would be obliged either to follow the lead of their ruler, or to move to another state. It was an arrangement which brought an end to religious warfare in Germany for several generations. But it was a landmark only as far as Lutheranism was concerned. Other Protestant groups were specifically excluded from the Peace of Augsburg. So the assumption is that the Lutherans were the only important Protestant group in Germany. This is untrue. An end date of 1555 also assumes that nothing of significance occurred after this time. This may have been generally true as far as the Lutherans were concerned, but it was clearly not the case with the Catholics or with other Protestant groups such as the Calvinists. The traditional dating of the Reformation in Germany is, therefore, an obvious example of the way in which the boundaries of the topic and the ways in which it should be studied have been unduly influenced by German historians with Lutheran sympathies. This should be kept in mind throughout the reading of this book. 'Structural' bias of this kind is often more difficult to detect than straightforward prejudice, and it is frequently much more important.

2 What was the Reformation?

> **KEY ISSUE** To what extent was the Reformation exclusively about religion?

Until about a quarter of a century ago historians found no difficulty in agreeing on a general definition of the Reformation. At the heart of this definition was the assumption that it was almost completely about religion. The Reformation was the term used to describe the complex set of events, lasting for most of the sixteenth century, by which a large minority of the membership of the Catholic Church changed allegiance and joined one of the new Protestant Churches which had set themselves up as rivals to the Church of Rome. It was seen as being made up of two related sets of events: the first, the early Reformation, taking place almost entirely in Germany and being centred on the life and activities of Martin Luther; and the second, the later Reformation, having its heartland in Switzerland, from which it spread far and wide, and revolving around the teachings of John Calvin. As a result of the Reformation the unity of western European Christendom was destroyed after having existed for more than a thousand years. This change was a major landmark in European history because it opened the door to widespread spiritual uncertainty. Whereas there had previously been only one set of beliefs that was widely accepted as correct, now there were quite a number. It was obvious to everybody that some of them must be wrong. Many began to wonder whether they all were.

This traditional, religion-centred definition of the Reformation did not, of course, totally ignore the political, social and economic dimensions of the changes that took place. It is more that these were viewed as peripheral rather than central. They therefore tended not to be studied directly, but rather to be brought in as 'added factors' or 'further consequences'. The important questions to ask were about the events that culminated in the 'break with Rome', about the ways in which the teachings of the religious reformers differed from those of the Catholic Church, and about the spread, organisation and structure of the newly created Protestant churches. Of course, such questions are of great significance, especially when acquiring an initial understanding of the topic. But they are not the issues upon which most historical research is currently concentrating. This is not because the religion-centred approach has been fully researched, leaving nothing new to be found out - although it is tempting to think that this is the case with Luther, about whom literally thousands of books have already been written - but because increasing numbers of historians have wished to challenge the assumption that the Reformation is essentially about religion.

No one, of course, denies that the Reformation took the form of changes in religious belief, practices and organisation. What is questioned is whether 'that is what it was really all about'. Were the changes wished for and welcomed for spiritual reasons or for more materialistic reasons? Were the most significant effects of the changes to be found in religion or in other aspects of life? Some historians have claimed that the Reformation can only be understood properly by recognising that it was essentially a social revolution. These writers have argued that in Germany, for example, the development and spread of Lutheranism occurred only because large elements of the population, especially the relatively prosperous townspeople, deeply resented the way in which the Church laid down strict rules on the detail of their daily lives, for example, regulations on fasting. Many of the people who embraced the reformed religion, therefore, were doing so largely in the expectation that they were freeing themselves from petty restrictions and so would be able to arrange their lives more as they wished. Religious beliefs and styles of worship were only of secondary importance. The primary aim was to destroy the social control exercised by the Church.

Other historians have maintained that the Reformation in Germany was essentially political in nature. At one level the Reformation has been seen as an early example of German nationalism, in effect being a mass movement of people refusing to accept the continuation of a situation in which foreigners, especially Italians living in Rome, controlled so many aspects of life in Germany, and milked the country of so much of its wealth. At another level it is described as being a tool used by local rulers to exclude external influence from their territories. Lutheran princes gained control of the Church, rather than it being in the hands of the Pope in Rome. This meant that final decisions about legal matters involving such things as marriage and inheritance, as well as matters of a more directly religious nature, were now completely in their hands.

Yet other historians have argued that the Reformation was really a matter of economics. They suggest that a period of rapid inflation made people actively look for ways to reduce their financial burdens, and that they saw a break with Rome as a very good way of achieving this. From the lowly peasant, who wrongly imagined that he would no longer be required to pay tithes (the tax on agricultural produce, paid to the Church), to the prince, who foresaw the possibility of seizing Church lands, there was the prospect of financial gain. This, it is sometimes argued, is what caused such widespread support for the Reformation, and is what provides its real meaning.

All these interpretations rely on the Reformation being placed in a wider context, in which it is just one example of a more general trend that is discernible about the period. The widest context of all is supplied by those historians who view the Reformation as being part of the radical changes taking place in the way most people thought about life and existence, and the assumptions they made about it. The contrast is made between medieval and modern patterns of thought. The medieval way of thinking is typified as being based on certainty - certainty that God designed the world to be as it is, certainty that each individual's duty is to live out with acceptance and good grace the life that has been planned for him and certainty that those in authority are the spokesmen of God. Modern thought patterns are seen as being based on doubt - doubt that all the answers are known, doubt that 'truths' handed down from high authority are necessarily to be relied upon, and doubt that the individual is as helpless in the face of God's purpose as had previously been thought. The Reformation is seen as an example of these changes taking place. The 'Age of Discovery', in which Europeans explored the world that was previously unknown to them, and the 'Age of Science', in which attempts were made to find new answers to old questions, rather than relying on the wisdom handed down from the past, can also be seen as movements in this overall pattern of change.

All these ideas about the Reformation contain elements of the truth. To some extent the different answers result from the fact that historians are giving varying meanings to the question 'What was the Reformation?' Some of the answers are given from a present-day point of view, with the benefit of knowledge about a broad sweep of history, both before and after the Reformation. In this way, historians are able to suggest interpretations that link together trends in ways that would have been impossible for contemporaries. Other writers have attempted to identify what the events meant to the people of the time. It is, therefore, not surprising that different answers have been found. The fact that the Reformation affected millions of people in many different places and at different times also explains why it is possible to find several seemingly valid answers to the same question. There is so much evidence to draw on that it would be impossible for any one historian or team of historians to study it all, even if they devoted a lifetime to it.

All research on the Reformation has to be very selective. And in selecting, it is very easy to gather together evidence that points in one direction, and to leave out evidence that would support an opposite conclusion, even though this may not have been the historian's intention. Once an initial ¹.ypothesis has been formed from the first evidence studied it is then always possible to locate other supporting evidence from the mass of documentation that exists. With a topic as vast as the Reformation it will always be possible to devise new definitions and explanations, and to locate plenty of evidence to support them. But it will remain impossible to produce conclusive proof of the correctness of any particular interpretation. Nor will historians be able to prove that another interpretation is definitely wrong. So uncertainty will always remain, and judgements will need to be made with caution. But if explanations of the past are to be offered, historians must be prepared to adopt some definitions, if only provisionally. In writing this volume, the argument that, to the people of the time, the events of the German Reformation were essentially about religious issues has been accepted as the most convincing interpretation currently on offer. This decision has naturally dictated the selection of the issues to be discussed in the remainder of the book.

3 The Causes of the Reformation

> **KEY ISSUES** How do historians normally organise their thinking about causes? Why are causes almost always highly controversial?

When historians research any event from the past it is often said that they are interested in finding out about the 'three "c"s' - causes, course and consequences. Another way of saying the same thing is to suggest that they are interested in finding the answers to three questions: 'Why did the event happen?', 'What happened?', and 'What were the results of what happened?'. When causes are being explored there are several approaches which can be used. The most popular is to divide the possible causes into groups according to timescale. Three timescales are normally used - long-term, short-term and immediate. Long-term causes are often thought about as spanning decades and even centuries; short-term causes are rarely considered to span more than a few years at the most; and immediate causes are usually concerned with what happened hours, days or, at most, months before the event in question. Because it is frequently impossible to be exact about the extent of each of the timescales, it is helpful to bear in mind a definition of each one. Long-term causes can usefully be thought of as factors which explain why the event was likely to happen at some time; short-term causes are those causes which explain why the event happened at about the time it did; and immediate causes provide us with an explanation of why the event occurred exactly when it did. Besides identifying causes and arranging them according to a timescale, it is usual for writers to assess the relative importance of the factors they have chosen. Habitually, they do this by asking the same question of each factor: 'Would the event have happened if this factor had not been present?'. Where the answer to this question is 'No', the factor is given a high importance rating. Conversely, where the answer is 'Yes', the factor is given only marginal status. As you read the discussion of the causes of the Reformation in Germany which follows, attempt to make up your own mind about the relative importance of the factors covered. When doing this you might choose to place each factor in one of three categories: 'very important', 'important', and 'not very important'.

a) Long-Term Causes

> **KEY ISSUES** What factors have been considered by historians as possible long-term causes of the Reformation in Germany? Why has it proved so difficult to establish the relative importance of each potential cause? To what extent is our understanding of the long-term causes of the Reformation in Germany uncertain rather than certain?

i) The State of Religion

It follows from the decision to accept the argument that the Reformation was essentially about religious issues, that its long-term causes must largely be sought in the state of religion at the time. Those who view the Reformation as mainly having to do with social, political, economic or intellectual change would, of course, search for its causes primarily in those areas, although even they would have to consider religious issues carefully in order to explain why the Reformation took place within a religious framework. So, in the discussion that follows, the focus will be on religious matters.

It is difficult for those who have only lived in a secular society, where the framework for everyday thinking is often provided by the acquisition and consumption of material wealth, to understand what it means to live in a society that is founded on religion. Such societies do exist in the present day, for example in the Muslim and Hindu worlds, but are seldom to be found in the so-called Christian world. This was not the case 500 years ago when the societies of western Europe were very much based on religion. This was most clearly illustrated in three ways: in the different status attached to the various leaders in society; in the aims most people had in living their lives; and in their reactions to everyday situations.

We are used to there being one main power structure in British society, based on the democratically elected government. In the Europe of 1500 there were two: the civil power represented by a prince (the word used by historians to describe a secular ruler whatever actual title he or she bore - king and duke were the most common), and the ecclesiastical power wielded by the Church, led by the Pope in Rome. Both powers competed for precedence but neither was successful in dominating the other for long. Normally they both accepted that the only workable solution was for them to regard each other as near equals. So the ordinary person had two theoretical masters: the head of the state and the head of the Church. On a daily basis it was the lowest ranks of the two power structures, the bailiff and the priest, with whom ordinary people came into contact.

The typical German in the early sixteenth century, in common with most of the inhabitants of western Europe, was deeply interested in both 'this world' and 'the next world'. Child mortality was high, many women died in childbirth, surviving adults were old at 40, and only a tiny proportion of the population attained the Bible's anticipated life span of 70, 'three score years and ten'. It was no more than simple prudence, when the possibility of death lay around every corner, for people to pay particular attention to what was required to ensure that they would go on to eternal life (salvation). Life on earth was often miserably short. It was merely a brief interlude, compared with the rest of time. Only fools and the weak-willed were prepared to risk eternal damnation in order to enjoy the fleeting pleasures of sin. For many people the most significant motivating force in their lives was the desire to be certain of salvation, and for this they had to turn to the Church.

We live in a time when most of what happens to us, or around us, can be explained in rational terms - we understand that events which affect us have causes which can normally be identified. This provides us with great security in that a sense of order prevails in our lives. Four hundred years ago the opposite was the case. Often the only explanation available was that 'God willed' or that 'it was the work of the Devil'. Whenever a public or private disaster threatened - a drought, a plague, or civil disorder; a theft, a serious illness, or potential damage to crops, for example - the immediate reaction was to call upon divine assistance. This was not usually done by addressing God directly, for he was thought to be inaccessible to ordinary mortals. The approach must be via his representatives on earth, the clergy, or more normally via humanity's representatives in heaven, the saints. Everybody had a saint who was believed to be particularly prepared to intercede on their behalf. The saint might be the one on whose day they were born, and after whom they were named, or the one who was the patron of their trade or occupation, or of their district. For many people, especially women, the Virgin Mary was favoured as being particularly approachable and very influential. The 'cult of saints' was very much a part of everyday life. People carried tokens of their saints wherever they went, they prayed to them in church, they gave charitable gifts in their names, they made promises of future conduct, and they sometimes went on pilgrimages to places particularly associated with them, especially to places where relics of them were on show. It was almost universally believed that special favours, including salvation, could be 'bought' in this way by various 'good works'.

In recent years historians have attempted to investigate the validity of such generalised judgements on the state of religious life at the end of the Middle Ages. They have been particularly interested in trying to reach conclusions about the 'health' of religion. Was it on the decline, was it in a state of equilibrium, or was it the focus of new enthusiasm? The assumption has been that if a correct diagnosis could be made of 'the state of religion' at the time, answers would be found to the question of the causes of the Reformation. However, it has proved very difficult, as might be expected, to locate appropriate sources of information. The evidence that does remain is often restricted to small local areas, and is inconclusive because it only relates to limited aspects of religious behaviour. So, although it has been possible to conclude that the amount of money being given to charitable foundations, or the sums being left in wills for the celebration of masses for the dead, or the number of people attending church was increasing or decreasing in particular towns or districts, this does not add up to clear evidence in support of, or in contradiction to, the traditionally accepted generalisations about the state of religion in the late Middle Ages. Nor does evidence collected over a wider geographical area - such as the number of religious books and pamphlets published in Germany - lend itself to easier interpretation, because what is unknown is always more extensive than what is known. So there is always the possibility that the picture revealed by the available evidence is not typical. In interpreting the figures on the publication of religious material, for example, there are the twin problems of the newness of printing - making it impossible to compare the late fifteenth century with earlier times - and of deciding how relevant such evidence is in reaching conclusions about the more than 90 per cent of the population who could not read. All that can be said is that historians are right to be interested in finding out whether religion was becoming more or less important in the lives of people in the pre-Reformation period, because such information could be very helpful in identifying the long-term causes of the Reformation. However, it seems certain that their efforts will never allow us to come to very firm conclusions: the issue will always remain controversial.

Unfortunately, the information collected so far only allows it to be said that there is considerable evidence of both a decline and an increase in interest in formal religion. So it is impossible to claim with any degree of confidence either that the Reformation was caused by a general upsurge in enthusiasm for religion, or that it was a reaction to a general decline in religious fervour. Much more research needs to be done on this issue. Even then it will not be possible to give a definitive answer. But whatever the differences of opinion over the direction in which popular religion was going at the time, nobody has effectively challenged the view that beliefs and assumptions about religion permeated all aspects of late-medieval life. It is this that explains how it was possible for differences over religion to become central to the political history of sixteenth-century Europe, to an extent that would be inconceivable four centuries later.

ii) The Teachings and Practices of the Church
Although it adds further to the uncertainties over the long-term causes of the Reformation, it must also be said that in 1500 there was definitely no widespread discontent over the teachings and practices of the Church. It seems that most people believed that as long as they were baptised soon after birth, went to mass at least once per year throughout their adult life, and received 'extreme unction' (forgiveness of sins granted by a priest in God's name), shortly before death, they were guaranteed salvation as long as their sins were not too numerous. They accepted that they would probably be required to spend a number of years - possibly running into thousands - in purgatory making amends for sins that had never been confessed to a priest and that had, therefore, never been forgiven by God. But they were confident that purgatory, the waiting room for heaven whose occupants suffered minor torments, was bearable if unpleasant. It was certainly far preferable to hell where, it was believed, the occupants, the totally unrepentant sinners, suffered the continual torture of fire, while being tormented by sulphurous smells and the taunts of devils and demons.

There was little feeling that the Church did not provide the right answers, or that salvation was not accessible to all who were prepared to make the effort necessary to obtain it. It was felt that this was often somewhat laborious as the Church taught that eternal life was to be gained by what you did rather than by what you believed. But at least it was not a matter of living sin-free lives. This was generally recognised as being an unrealistic aspiration. What was required was that proper atonement for sins was made. This could be done by confessing sins to a priest and doing penance as directed; by regularly attending mass (the service containing the Eucharist in which the sacrifice of Jesus's life was re-enacted); or by a variety of 'good works'. One type of 'good work' was the purchase of indulgences. These were promises of a reduction in the time to be spent in purgatory. They were often stated as being remission of a set number of years, sometimes running into millions. Indulgences were sold on the authority of the Pope and were increasingly used as an additional method of raising revenue. Many rulers would not allow them to be sold in their territory because the system was open to abuse. However, on the whole, there is little evidence that ordinary people resented them. To them they seemed like a good bargain.

iii) The Structure and Organisation of the Church

There was, however, considerable resentment in Germany over aspects of the structure and organisation of the Church. Much of this ill-feeling came about because the Church was under the control of foreigners. It was headed by the Pope who lived in Rome and ruled over much of central Italy. Each Pope was elected for life by the Cardinals, the highest rank of clergy. Cardinals, in their turn, were chosen by the Pope. The large majority of Cardinals, and nearly every Pope, was Italian. This would have been of no great significance had it not been for the fact that the Papacy, needing to maintain its political position in the face of French and Habsburg attempts to dominate Italy, had an almost inexhaustible need for additional income. This it sought to acquire largely from Germany, the only part of Christendom that was both rich and lacking in a strong central government which could resist the financial demands of the Pope. Huge amounts of money, in the visible form of gold and silver, left Germany each year to go to Rome.

The Pope was able to demand this money largely because he was the only one able to grant permission to those who wished to be exempt from various of the legal requirements imposed by the Church. The largest sums were extracted from the German ruling families when they wished to purchase senior Church positions for their younger sons. The amount was especially large if the child was under-age, or already held one such position, because such appointments were illegal and required special papal dispensation before they could take place. With about one-fifth of Germany under the control of virtually independent bishops and archbishops, there was plenty of scope for such lucrative dealings. This was especially the case with the archbishoprics of Mainz, Cologne and Trier, whose incumbents were also members of the elite group of seven Electors which chose the Emperor of the Holy Roman Empire. Smaller, but not insignificant, sums were obtained from all newly appointed churchmen, and from laymen who required special rulings, normally in matters relating to marriage and inheritance, the two major areas over which the Church had gained legal control. The financial dealings of the rich had an immediate effect, of course, on the common people. Whatever money was to be paid to the Pope had to be raised by extracting it, often by questionable means, from the population at large. Thus the demands of the papacy were a matter of general concern. The early reformers made much of the fact that the Pope, who was meant to be the good shepherd, devoted much of his energy to fleecing his flock.

The grasping nature of the papacy tended to be mirrored at all levels of the Church in Germany. The major interest of the clergy seemed to be the acquisition of wealth rather than the spiritual welfare of the population. It was not the fact that the churchmen were worldly that caused the resentment: it was more that they overcharged for whatever they did, leaving the layman to pay or risk damnation. There was therefore widespread anticlericalism (hostility to the Church and those who held posts in it), which created an atmosphere in which any attack on the Church's hierarchy was likely to be generally welcomed. It was against this background of financial exploitation that the other shortcomings of the Church were viewed.

iv) The Papacy

Modern Protestant writers have tended to be highly critical of the early sixteenth-century papacy because of its low moral tone. The Popes of the period - especially the notorious Rodrigo Borgia, whose reign as Alexander VI from 1492-1503 was the most shameful of all, making the name of Borgia synonymous with murder, sexual licence and almost every known vice - were generally cynical politicians who were more interested in satisfying their personal whims and furthering their family fortunes than in protecting even the political interests of the papacy. Spiritual concerns were very low on their order of priorities, unless they represented some threat to their financial interests. They openly committed most of 'the deadly sins', and sometimes even ridiculed the religious practices they were expected to uphold. But there is little evidence that this behaviour, even when it became widely known in Germany in the 1520s, actually caused great dissatisfaction. In this, the Protestant historians have overstated the case. It has not been established that the faults of the papacy were in any real sense a cause of the Reformation. Their importance was that the Pope and his advisers were so busy interpreting events in terms of their own worldly interests that they failed to see the spiritual significance of what was happening until it was too late to prevent a split in the Church.

v) Abuses within Germany

Similarly, the widespread so-called abuses within the Church in Germany have been of greater concern to historians than they were to the people of the time. Most higher clergy were members of the nobility with little education and no theological training, who viewed their posts as sources of power, prestige and income. Many parish priests, especially in remote rural areas, were illiterate peasants who hardly knew how to perform the normal church services. Pluralism (the holding of more than one post as a parish priest, bishop, etc.), and the resulting absenteeism, were common, with untrained curates often employed to take the place of absent priests. But this was unremarkable to the majority of a population that knew no better, although there is some evidence that the lack of spiritual support was felt in some quarters, particularly in the towns where it became common for special preachers to be appointed, whose duty it was to provide regular sermons to teach the people what they should believe - a responsibility which many parish priests were unwilling or unable to undertake. Yet it seems that the state of the Church in general, although deplorable to modern eyes, was not a matter of great concern to the average citizen of early sixteenth-century Germany. It cannot be argued, therefore, that it was a major or direct cause of the Reformation. At most it can be contended that the situation weakened the Church and made it more difficult for it to defend itself effectively once it came under heavy attack.

So the search for certain and clearly identifiable long-term causes of the Reformation is somewhat frustrating. All that can be found are situations and possible trends that made it likely that any attacks on the Church would be well received in many quarters, especially in Germany.

b) Short-Term Causes

> **KEY ISSUE** How far is it possible to argue that the work of the humanists was the main short-term cause of the Reformation?

i) The Humanists

Unfortunately, even when possible short-term causes are investigated the situation is not a great deal clearer. Traditional explanations of the short-term causes of the Reformation tend to start by examining the work of the humanists. The humanists were scholars who were particularly interested in studying the writings of ancient Greece and Rome, as well as the Bible, in as near an original text as possible. Their aim was to discover the meaning that the author had initially intended, rather than accepting interpretations that had been made in the Middle Ages based on incomplete texts and poor translations. Humanism had become increasingly important in the scholarly world of the highly educated during the fifteenth century as the Renaissance had spread northwards from its birthplace in Italy. At its heart was a belief that life in this world need not be viewed largely as a penance to be served by sinful men before their souls could obtain entry to heaven. Rather than meekly accepting established teachings and explanations, the humanists demanded to be shown the evidence. This approach to issues was generally unwelcome in the Church, where the normal requirement was unquestioning obedience. But not all prominent churchmen were hostile to it, because it could be argued that by looking at the evidence afresh one might be able to come to a clearer understanding of God and his will. So the humanists were allowed to continue their researches unmolested as long as they did nothing to challenge the existing power structure within the Church.

In the early sixteenth century the leading humanist scholar was Desiderius Erasmus (1466?-1536). From his home in the Netherlands he built up a network of correspondents in many countries via which the latest scholarly findings were widely circulated and the issues of the day discussed. His advice was sought by many of Europe's leading political figures. His publications were written in Latin, the language of scholars, and were to be found in all centres of learning throughout western Europe. His reputation as a thinker and researcher was unsurpassed. His speciality was the study of the New Testament of the Bible, and in this he showed the typical humanist approach. He was not prepared to rely on the generally accepted text - the Vulgate, which was a translation into Latin of the original texts - but insisted on studying the earliest known manuscripts, which were in Greek. He drew attention to the ways in which some of the Church's teachings were based on texts that were in fact mistranslations made by St. Jerome, the author of the Vulgate. One of his great contributions was to publish, in 1516, an accurate version of the New Testament in Greek, which other scholars could use in preparing vernacular editions of the Bible (editions in their own languages). He worked to make it clear to those with the education and intellectual ability to understand, that the teachings and practices of the Church were riddled with errors and inconsistencies. He felt particularly strongly that the Church should be encouraging people to live Christ-like lives rather than teaching them to seek salvation through the practice of empty formalities. In this he was echoing the views of a large but unorganised band of reformers throughout Europe which had been seeking a spiritual regeneration of the Church for at least a century.

Given his views on how Christians should act, it is not surprising that Erasmus launched attacks on what he saw as the godlessness of many of the higher clergy. His satire, *In Praise of Folly*, in which he ridiculed the typical churchman by appearing to praise him for his faults, became the contemporary equivalent of a best seller. By the time Luther became famous there were thousands of followers and admirers of Erasmus in all parts of Europe, many of whom were in high places.

Historians have tended to see the existence of so much support for the idea of reform in the years before 1517 as one of the major short-term causes of the Reformation. In fact, it was even said by contemporaries that 'Erasmus laid the egg and Luther hatched it'. Unfortunately, the link between Erasmus and his followers and the Reformation is not so clear-cut. In fact, Erasmus and many of the other leading humanists refused to join Luther, preferring to remain within the Church and to campaign for change from within. They denied that they were in any sense responsible for what they thought of as Luther's excesses. Erasmus's retort that 'I laid a hen's egg, but what Luther hatched was a bird of a quite different sort', typifies this attitude. In 1520 he wrote to the Papal Legate saying that:

1   The corruption of the Roman Court may require reform, extensive and immediate, but I and the like of me are not called on to take a work like that upon ourselves. I would rather see things left as they are than to see a revolution which may lead to one knows not what. Others may
5   be martyrs if they like. I aspire to no such honour. Some hate me for being a Lutheran; some for not being a Lutheran. You may assure yourself that Erasmus has been, and always will be, a faithful subject of the Roman See.

This was to remain his position throughout the rest of his life. Two years later in a letter to one of his many correspondents he further clarified his position:

1   Each side pushes me and each reproaches me. My silence against Luther is interpreted as consent, while the Lutherans accuse me of having deserted the gospel out of timidity. ... I cannot be other than what I am, and cannot but execrate dissension. I cannot but love peace and
5   concord. I see how much easier it is to start than to assuage a tumult.

Luther thought such a view was completely unacceptable, and was not slow to inform Erasmus of his opinion in very strong language. The two men rapidly lost respect for one another, and, in Luther's case, admiration turned to hatred. Erasmus's feelings were not as strong, but even he allowed his annoyance to show, as in this letter to Luther:

1   The whole world knows your nature, according to which you have guided your pen against no one more bitterly and, what is more odious, more maliciously, than against me. ... How do your scurrilous charges that I am an atheist help the argument? ... Wish me any curse you will
5   except your temper, unless the Lord change it for you.

Erasmus's views were shared by many humanists. Some, such as Sir Thomas More in England, were even prepared to die rather than renounce their allegiance to the Church. So it is difficult to argue that the Reformation took place directly as a result of the activities of the humanists. But at least it is possible to show that their work helped to create an intellectual climate in which the teachings of Luther were likely to be acceptable. It can therefore be said that, had it not been for the work of Erasmus and his fellow humanists, the Reformation would probably not have happened. Although it was not their intention, they helped create an intellectual climate in which Luther's ideas would be acceptable.

ii) Earlier Reformers

Some historians have not wished to answer the general question 'Why did the Reformation take place?' They have been more interested in trying to work out why it happened where and when it did, instead of occurring in another place at another time. Point is given to their enquiries by the fact that there had been previous challenges to the established authority of the Church. These had paralleled Luther's actions in many ways, but none of them had resulted in the permanent creation of rival churches. The two reformers who are normally seen as being Luther's precursors are John Wycliffe (1320?-84) and John Huss (1368-1415). Wycliffe in England and Huss in Bohemia (part of the modern Czech Republic) had spoken out against both the abuses within the structure and organisation of the Church, and the teachings of the Church which seemed to be in contradiction to the intentions of God as revealed in the Bible. Luther was to do likewise. Wycliffe and Huss attracted large numbers of supporters who were even prepared to die for their new-found faith. Luther did the same. But Wycliffe's followers, the Lollards, were never able to establish a separate identity, although they remained an identifiable strand within the Church in England for several generations. Huss's supporters, the Hussites, were somewhat more successful, particularly after his arrest and execution as a heretic while under the Emperor's safe conduct. They gained control of the Church in some, particularly remote, parts of Bohemia, and managed to maintain their position, protecting themselves from effective reprisals. But they were not able to go on to the offensive and win over new areas to their beliefs. Yet Luther's followers were able to do this.

Why was there this difference? Why did Luther's attempts to reform the Church lead to the Reformation whereas Wycliffe's and Huss's did not? After all, they all lived at times when there were widespread abuses in the Church, and they all attracted large bodies of supporters. Part of the answer would seem to lie in the personalities, characters, and abilities of the reformers, and in the environment in which they had to operate. These issues are at the heart of the chapters that follow.

iii) Immediate Causes

Whereas historians disagree violently among themselves about both the long-term and the short-term causes of the Reformation in Germany, there is little dispute about the immediate causes. There is widespread agreement that these were provided by the actions of Martin Luther in the years between 1517 and 1521, and by the reactions of those in authority to what he did. These events are explored in detail in the next chapter.

Summary Diagram
The background to the Reformation

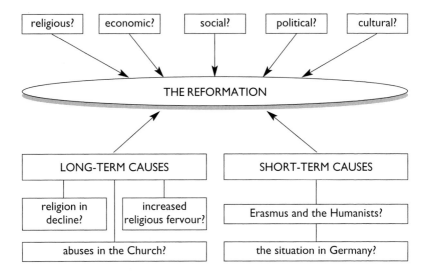

religious? economic? social? political? cultural?

THE REFORMATION

LONG-TERM CAUSES   SHORT-TERM CAUSES

religion in decline?   increased religious fervour?   Erasmus and the Humanists?

abuses in the Church?   the situation in Germany?

Working on Chapter 1

If you are near the beginning of your history course, you will probably have found this chapter quite difficult. This is only to be expected and should not be a cause for concern. If this is your situation, now is *not* the time to continue battling with the ideas you have just encountered. Your best bet would be to move straight on to the next chapter which you should find much more straightforward. However, at some stage you will need to reach your own conclusions on the issues you have been reading about. This is especially the case with the issue of the causes of the Reformation. The best time to do this would probably be when you have read the rest of the book.

If you are a significant way into your course you should be prepared to work further on the chapter straight away. Most of this work is likely to be thinking, but it would certainly be helpful if you were to write down in your own words the conclusions you come to. Possibly the most productive way of spending your time would be to work through the chapter again, copying down the questions in the issues boxes as you come across them. By writing brief answers to each question you will be making sure you have carried out the thinking necessary. You may need to read parts of the chapter several times before you are able to reach a conclusion that satisfies you. An alternative approach would be to use the summary diagram as the framework for what you write. Each box could be used as a heading. Memorising the diagram would then be a useful part of exam preparation.

Answering structured and essay questions on Chapter 1

Most questions on this topic are, in essence, asking 'What were the causes of the Reformation?'. If the paper you are sitting is made up of two- or three-part structured questions you may find this actual wording being used. There might then be two or three headings provided to indicate how your answer should be structured. Look at the following example:

a) Explain the long-term and the short-term causes of the Reformation in Germany.

b) What was the significance of the part played by Martin Luther?

What is the implication of 'explain' rather than 'describe' being used as the first word in the question? It is important to remember that marks will be given both for the factual content of your answer and for the analytical skills you display.

If you are sitting a paper which requires you to write full essay answers you will rarely find a question on the causes of the Reformation in a straightforward form. This is because most examiners aim to give you an opportunity to show how well you can think under pressure, rather than testing whether you can regurgitate your notes. So questions are normally wrapped up in a way that requires you to disentangle the real meaning.

A technique frequently used by examiners is to select one possible cause and to ask '*to what extent*' it explains the Reformation. Typical examples are:

1. To what extent was the Reformation the result of the internal weaknesses of the Church in the early sixteenth century?

2. To what extent could the Reformation be explained as an expansion of the Renaissance?

Do not be put off if you do not know much about the 'possible cause' mentioned in the question. You will be able to manage as long as you understand what it means (the 'expansion of the Renaissance' refers to the work of the humanists), and can think of two or three things to say about it. What is important is that you have four or five interesting points to make on the issue of the causes of the Reformation.

All '*to what extent*' questions can be tackled in the same way.

1. Start with a brief introductory paragraph explaining the approach you are going to take. There are three main ways of answering questions on *causes* or *effects/results*. You can organise your points either as *conditional* and *contingent* causes/effects, as *long-term*, *short-term*, and *immediate* causes/effects, or as *political*, *economic*, *social*, etc., causes/effects. It is probably easiest to use the former structure with questions on the causes of the Reformation.

2. In the second paragraph explain the ways in which the cause mentioned in the title was important. Make a judgement about the significance of the cause. Was it the most important, very important, not very important? You must be clear about the criteria you are going to use when you make judgments on significance or importance. For example, you could decide that for a cause to be important it should be a *necessary* cause (ie, that the event would not have happened without it) or that other causes should be dependent on it.

3. In each of the following paragraphs discuss one of your 'sets' of causes. In what order will you present your paragraph points? You should have a good reason for the order you have chosen.

4. Leave time for a brief concluding paragraph. Use this to make clear the relative significance you attach to each of the points you have made and, if possible, make your final sentence memorable in some way. It is often an advantage for a fine phrase or a stimulating idea to be left with the examiner, just as his or her thoughts are turning to the mark or grade you are to be awarded!

Source-based questions on Chapter 1

1. Erasmus and the Reformation

Read the extracts from three of Erasmus's letters given on page 16. Answer the following questions:

a) In the first and second extracts, what reasons does Erasmus give for remaining a Catholic. *(5 marks)*

b) What impression of Luther is given in the third extract? *(3 marks)*

c) Using evidence from all three extracts, describe what seem to be the salient features of Erasmus's character. *(6 marks)*

d) What are the strengths and weaknesses of these extracts in showing what Erasmus actually thought and felt? *(6 marks)*

With sets of questions such as the above, make sure that you take advantage of the fact that you have been told how many marks are allocated for each part. Almost without exception, you should plan the amount of time you spend on each part directly in proportion to the number of marks available for it. Thus, for example, you should expect to spend twice as much time on each of parts **c)** and **d)** as you do on part **b)**.

In general terms, you can expect that an examiner will require you to make as many points as there are marks available for the question. For example, it would be reasonable for you to think that in answering part **d)** you should mention three strengths and three weaknesses if you are to gain maximum credit.

2 Luther's Revolt, 1517-21

POINTS TO CONSIDER

This chapter describes the stages by which Martin Luther became a rebel against the authority of the Church. As you read the chapter for the first time there are two main jobs for you to do. You need to learn about the six main events - you will find them in the Key Dates list below - which led to this happening, and you need to identify the motives of Luther and of the Pope for acting as they did.

KEY DATES

31 October 1517	Luther pinned *Ninety-five Theses* against the sale of indulgences to the door of the main church in Wittenberg
April 1518	Luther justified his arguments at the Convention of the Augustinian Order
October 1518	Luther met with Cardinal Cajetan at Augsburg
July 1519	18 day formal disputation with Johan Eck at Leipzig
June 1520	Bull of Excommunication, *'Exsurge Domine'*
April 1521	Diet of Worms

1 Introduction

> **KEY ISSUE** Why is it important to recognise the prejudice or point of view you already hold when you begin a study of Luther and the German Reformation?

Most of us are used to the sensationalised news story. In the tabloid press, especially, editors and journalists seem to feel the need to over dramatise. The contribution of the individual is focused on - the human interest angle - and in the process is often blown up out of all proportion. Concentration is on the aspects of the story that are likely to appeal to the interests or emotions of the audience. Complicating factors are ignored as getting in the way of the main story line. The end result is often something that is memorable but that is in no way an accurate reflection of what actually happened. There is a real temptation to adopt the same approach in describing the beginnings of the Reformation in Germany.

All the ingredients required for a good story are present. There is a larger than life character, Martin Luther, a monk who has taken the vow of obedience but who rebels against the Head of the Church.

There is plenty of corruption in high places, accompanied by evidence of irregular sexual practices. There are possibilities of following popular themes - the weak struggling successfully against the strong; the good overcoming the bad; or the darkness of ignorance being dispelled by the light of understanding. Great care is needed if the dangers of viewing the events with the perspective of the twentieth century or through the filter of one's own prejudices are to be avoided.

This danger is as real for research historians and the authors of text books as it is for sixth form and college students. Nobody approaches the Reformation story from a standpoint of neutrality. For those brought up in an active Christian tradition, even if church attendance is infrequent, there is a side to identify with - either Catholic or Protestant - even before any evidence is studied. However hard the student or historian who has been brought up in contact with organised Christian religion tries to be unbiased, there are likely to be times when a basic assumption that one side or the other is fundamentally in the right will show through. Nor is it easy for the non-Christian, the agnostic or the atheist to study the Reformation from a neutral position. Even if there is no inbuilt prejudice to overcome, there is likely to be a natural inclination to favour either the rebel or the forces of established authority, either the underdog or the side expected to win, either the idealist or the pragmatist In no book on the Reformation is the author able to write without his or her point of view playing a part. Very often it is painfully obvious in the judgements that are made. So it is possible to identify a 'Catholic school' and a 'Protestant school' of historians who have studied Martin Luther.

Not all historians belong to one of these two schools, but those who do not are not automatically more reliable just because their prejudices are less obvious. Readers studying Martin Luther should make a conscious effort to identify the point of view of each author with whom they come into contact, and should then attempt to make the necessary allowances when deciding how far to accept the interpretation put forward. There are no exceptions to this rule - not even the present volume.

Naturally it follows that you, the reader, are unlikely to begin a study of Martin Luther without at least a tentative judgement of the man in your mind. You should be aware of what this is, and should be careful not to fall into the trap of gathering information that supports your view and ignoring that which seems to challenge it. Of course, this is not to suggest that having a point of view is somehow wrong or reprehensible. What is to be avoided is the point of view that is never explicitly recognised, and therefore is never questioned or modified in the light of fresh evidence. Having a point of view is unavoidable, even when compiling what appears to be a straightforward factual narrative, such as that which follows. There may be no clearly judgmental statements to help you identify what this is, but the selection of one event as more worthy of inclusion than another depends on a prior judgement about what is significant and what is not. This in turn will be closely linked with the author's point of view.

2 The Origins of the Revolt

a) The Ninety-five Theses

Between the years 1517 and 1521 the actions of Martin Luther (1483-1546) shook the foundations of the Catholic Church, and threatened to shatter the medieval concept of Christendom. After 1521 there was a real possibility that the 'Church united' would not survive. This situation was not the outcome of a pre-planned series of attacks that was designed to have this result. It was just that one thing led to another until eventually there was no going back, and the only way forward was schism (the division of the Church into several Churches). It was as much a matter of events controlling people as of people controlling events.

As with many major events in history, the beginnings of Luther's revolt against Rome were relatively trivial. On the eve of All Saints' Day, 31 October 1517, he pinned *Ninety-five Theses* against the sale of indulgences to the door of the main church in Wittenberg, the capital of electoral Saxony. (A generation earlier the state of Saxony had been divided in two - electoral Saxony ruled over by an Elector, and ducal Saxony ruled over by a Duke.) The theses were in Latin and were mainly intended to be a contribution to the academic debate on the subject. The fact that they were pinned to the church door was in no way unusual. Such an action was an accepted way of 'going public' with a point of view in the days before learned journals, in which such papers would nowadays appear. What was a little pointed was the timing of the action. The *Ninety-five Theses* appeared a few hours before the one day in the year on which the Elector of Saxony sold indulgences to those who visited his famous collection of relics. Luther clearly intended his arguments to receive wide publicity.

At the time Luther was a professor at the recently founded University of Wittenberg. His particular interest was the Bible, about which he had been lecturing at the University since he had been sent there in 1511. Like many academics of his time, Luther was a monk and as such was compelled to serve where his superiors directed him. But he was in no way a dry intellectual like so many of his colleagues. He was driven by a remarkably strong inner force which gave him no peace as long as he remained in doubt about the exact nature of God and of his relationship to humanity. This had been the most important element in his life ever since he had become a monk at the age of 21 in fulfilment of a promise he had made to St Anne, his patron saint, for protecting him when struck by a thunderbolt during a storm.

Although he had not yet come to a complete understanding about these things, he had come a long way since the time when, as a young monk, he had feared God as a figure of vengeance who punished humanity in eternity for every sin committed in the earthly life. He was already convinced that the Church's teachings on these matters were fundamentally incorrect. The orthodox view was that salvation was to be gained by being 'sin-free' at the time of death. This could be assured by wiping out in the eyes of God all the sins that had been committed during life. It was almost a book-keeping exercise. Enough 'merit' had to be acquired to counterbalance the sins. Merit could be gained by 'good works', including the purchase of indulgences. In contrast, Luther believed that salvation was freely offered by God to everybody. All that was necessary to acquire it was to have faith - complete trust in God. Good works were not only ineffectual in gaining salvation: they could even lead to damnation if they were looked upon as a substitute for faith.

So Luther did not regard disagreements over such matters as the sale of indulgences as merely matters of theological debate. To him it was a question of eternal life and death. He had seen people continue to sin because they felt secure from damnation once they had bought an indulgence which promised them forgiveness for all sins

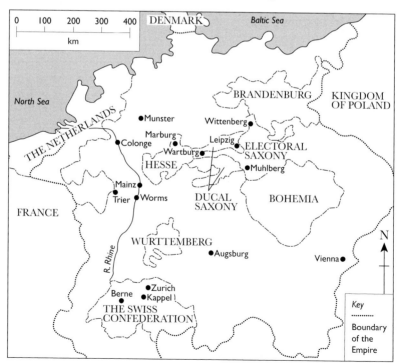

The Holy Roman Empire in the early sixteenth century.

committed during their lifetime, whether past or future. He was convinced that these people were being fatally misled by the Church, and his conscience would not allow him to sit back and do nothing.

b) John Tetzel and Albert, Archbishop of Mainz

The issue had been brought to a head by the activities of John Tetzel, a Dominican friar. Tetzel was selling indulgences in the area near to Wittenberg. He was not allowed into the territories of the Elector for fear that he would compete with the indulgences sold in Wittenberg. This was a particularly real fear because Tetzel was selling the most 'powerful' indulgences ever offered. Not only could they assure forgiveness for all the sins of the purchaser, they could even secure the release from purgatory (see page 12) of the soul of a friend or relative who was already dead. In his sermons, which were little more than exhortations to buy, Tetzel appealed to his audiences to prove how much they loved their dead parents or children by giving them the most precious gift of all. The jingle ran:

> 'As soon as the coin in the coffer rings,
> The soul from purgatory springs.'

Tens of thousands of people, including many from Wittenberg who made special journeys to reach Tetzel, invested their savings in indulgences. It was with these events especially in mind that Luther wrote his *Ninety-five Theses*.

Luther hoped that the arguments contained in his theses would convince the Archbishop of Mainz, under whose authority Tetzel was operating, that the sale of indulgences should be halted. He therefore sent him a copy of the *Ninety-five Theses*, along with a covering letter in which he explained why he was so concerned.

1 I do not complain so much of the loud cry of the preacher of Indulgences, which I have not heard, but regret the false meaning which the simple folk attach to it, the poor souls believing that when they have purchased such letters they have secured their salvation, also, that the
5 moment the money jingles in the box souls are delivered from purgatory, and that all sins will be forgiven through a letter of indulgence ... And, lastly, that through these Indulgences the man is freed from all penalties! Ah, dear God! Thus are those souls which have been committed to your care, dear father, being led in the paths of death, and
10 for them you will be required to render an account.

The Archbishop, Albert of Brandenburg, was disturbed by this potential threat to his plans. He was relying on the money raised from the sale of indulgences to pay off the debts he had incurred in securing the agreement of the Pope to his acquisition of the Archbishopric, although it was popularly believed that the money collected was to be used to finance the rebuilding of St Peter's

Cathedral in Rome. Albert was still in his early twenties and had had no theological training, but he had already bought his way into a bishopric and two archbishoprics, each of which carried with it large territories over which he was the sole ruler. In the process he had become one of the most powerful princes in Germany.

Albert felt greatly threatened by Luther, whose *Ninety-five Theses* were rapidly translated into German, printed, and widely distributed. They struck a chord with many people. Those who understood theology recognised the strength of Luther's attack on the very nature of indulgences, while the untrained, but serious-minded, majority of the population were re-awakened in their resentment at the way in which the poor of Germany were constantly forced, tricked or cajoled into paying money to the Church, much of which found its way to a

'John Tetzel put to flight by the mighty hero Luther' is the title of this broadsheet showing Tetzel selling indulgences.

foreigner - the Pope in Rome. Luther's appeal to the sentiments of ordinary Germans was clear:

1 Christians should be taught that, unless they abound in possessions beyond their needs, their duty is to retain what is necessary for their own household, and in no way to squander it in buying pardons.
Christians should be taught that the purchase of pardons is voluntary
5 not obligatory.
Christians should be taught that in granting pardons, the Pope has more need, and more desire, for devout prayer on his own behalf than for ready money …
Christians should be taught that, if the Pope knew the exactions of the
10 preachers of Indulgences, he would rather have the basilica of St Peter reduced to ashes than built with the skin, flesh and bones of his sheep.

3 Attempts to Silence Luther

> **KEY ISSUES** What steps were taken to silence Luther between 1518 and 1520? Why were they not successful?

a) Cardinal Cajetan

Albert immediately appealed to the Pope for support, requesting that Luther be silenced. The reaction of the Pope, Leo X (1513-21), was swift, given the great distances over which correspondence had to travel. It was decided that Luther should be dealt with through the structure of the Augustinian order of monks to which he belonged. In April 1518 he attended the triennial convention of his order and attempted to justify his actions. His stance was generally supported, to the Pope's great embarrassment. Pope Leo now decided to take matters into his own hands. Luther was ordered to come to Rome. He refused. In an attempt to persuade him to see reason, a papal representative, Cardinal Cajetan, was sent to Germany. He summoned Luther to meet him in Augsburg in October 1518, and for several days attempted to convince him of the errors of his ways. What started as an exercise in sweet reason rapidly deteriorated into an attempt to coerce Luther by threats. Cajetan made it clear that papal patience was nearly exhausted and that dire punishments would follow if Luther did not retract what he had written.

Luther remained unmoved. His position had been clearly stated from the outset, and his conscience would not allow him to change it. He argued that he had identified mistakes in the Church's teachings. He could only abandon his point of view if he could either be shown evidence from the Bible which proved him wrong, or be convinced of his errors by 'sound reason'. The Church's position was equally clear. It maintained that it was for the Pope alone to interpret the Bible and to decide upon the teachings of the Church. The duty of all Catholics was to obey him as God's representative on earth. The Church therefore had no need to convince anybody of anything. It merely had to insist on good discipline. Thus the two sides were arguing at cross purposes with no real point of contact.

b) The Leipzig Disputation

After Cajetan's unsuccessful mission the papal authorities were persuaded at last that their strategy was misguided. They were offering no defence to Luther's charges and were leaving the way clear for him to gain ever-increasing numbers of supporters in Germany. Papal credibility was so low that the traditional appeal to unthinking obedience was being rejected. So it was decided to meet Luther's challenge in open debate. A formal disputation of the accepted academic type was arranged to take place in Leipzig during July 1519. Doctor Johann Eck was chosen to uphold the Church's position. He was recognised as being the most skilful debater in Germany. For 18 days the issues were argued before a panel of 'neutral' academics, in the presence of local dignitaries. Eck undoubtedly won the competition, but only in technical terms. He scored numerous debating points, trapping Luther and his Wittenberg supporters into putting forward some indefensible arguments. But he convinced nobody of the validity of his case, for it was impossible for cold logic to overcome what had now become fervently held beliefs. Although Eck behaved after the disputation as if he were the undisputed victor, unbiased observers were able to see that the outcome was very different.

Luther had come to Leipzig with the reputation of being a rebel. He departed under suspicion of being a revolutionary. Eck was responsible for the change. He had forced Luther to take each of his arguments to its logical conclusion. So what had been a challenge to the Pope on matters of detail became a general contention that the individual believer studying the Bible with God's guidance was as likely to discover the truth about divine will as was the leader of the Church. What had been a suggestion that the Pope was exceeding his powers was now a claim that the Pope had no special powers at all. Where the people associated with Luther had thought themselves to be seeking the reform of abuses, it was now clear to all but the unrealistically optimistic that there was no possibility of the reformers reaching an agreement with the established Church authorities. Early in the disputation Eck had attempted to label Luther as a Hussite (see page 17) in an effort to discredit him in the eyes of the German princes. By the end of the debate Luther was proudly proclaiming himself to be in agreement on all important points with his Czech predecessor who had been declared a heretic and had been burned for his beliefs.

c) Bull of Excommunication

Following the Leipzig Disputation, Pope Leo X considered that Luther had revealed himself to be so extreme that it would now be safe to proceed against him with the full force of the Church's authority. This would be done by sending him a legal document, a bull, informing him that he was an outcast from the Church and that all obedient Christians would refuse to have any dealings with him. To ensure that this was known, the Bull of Excommunication would be read from the pulpit of every church. The Bull of Excommunication, known as was customary by its first words, *Exsurge Domine*, was issued in June 1520. Luther showed his contempt for the Pope by burning the Bull publicly. The breach was now complete.

4 Luther's Standpoint

> **KEY ISSUE** What were the implications of Luther becoming an evangelical, believing that the Bible was the only source of Christian truth?

How had what seemed to start as a minor disagreement grown to such proportions? Much of the answer lies in an understanding of Luther's motivation. He was not interested in acquiring power or riches, nor even in establishing a public reputation for himself as an outstanding theologian. He was in no way a politician. He could therefore not be swayed by arguments that focused on the consequences of his actions - on what others might think, say or do as a result of the stand he was taking. He did not really mind whether he lived or died. He was impervious to the factors that influence most people's actions, such as the desires to be happy, rich, famous, loved, approved of, successful or, merely, to survive.

His interests were selfish but were truly other-worldly. His overriding concern was with his own salvation. In common with many people of his own and earlier ages, he recognised that one's earthly life was likely to be painful and short. Sickness and death were commonplace and constantly gave reminders of the transient nature of the body and other material things. What mattered was the soul. It had the potential for eternal life, against which the few years spent on earth were insignificant. But the soul's future life (salvation), could only be assured if its 'owner', while on earth, acted in the way laid down by God. In his early years he had accepted the orthodox view that the Church's teachings showed what was necessary. From the time he became a monk in 1505 at the age of 21, he devoted his whole being to carrying out what he understood to be God's instructions. Yet the more he tried the more he became convinced that the task was impossible. He became deeply depressed about his own inadequacy.

He grew to hate the God who seemed to be playing a terrible game with humanity - making rules that doomed the players to automatic failure, and then condemning them to an eternity in hell. But in his despair he did not think to challenge what he had been taught.

The breakthrough came with his increasing study of the Bible. He became convinced that here, rather than in the teachings of the Church, lay the true revelation of God's will. As he struggled to unravel its meaning, he realised in a flash of inspiration that salvation was secured by what you believed and not by what you did. He no longer saw God as the terrible judge who weighed each life in the balance and rejected those he found wanting, but rather as the God of love who was freely offering salvation to all who would believe in Him and in his son, Jesus Christ He interpreted the force of the phrase 'by faith are ye saved' as being 'by faith alone are ye saved'. So the Latin phrase *sola fide* (by faith alone) became the central idea of Luther's thinking. Now, for the first time in his life, he was certain that he was saved.

Having made this discovery, his period of personal agony was over. But the implications of the discovery needed to be worked through. It was in this context that the issue of indulgences became so important, because their efficacy, as claimed by John Tetzel, depended upon the assumption that salvation was to be gained by building up enough merit in God's eyes to counterbalance one's accumulated tally of sin. Once it was accepted that 'good works' were a *sign* of being saved rather than the *cause* of it, it was impossible to attach any value to indulgences except as remission from earthly penalties imposed by the Church. This was the stance that Luther took in his *Ninety-five Theses*.

Thus what may have appeared to be a disagreement over a minor, and relatively recent, practice of the Church, was actually the result of differences on matters of fundamental importance. There was no possibility that Luther, given his total personal commitment to the idea of *sola fide*, would be prepared to give ground, and the Church was such a complex structure of vested interests that it did not possess the machinery to introduce such a major change in its pattern of beliefs, even had the political will existed to do so. So a collision course was inevitable from the outset.

What made the conflict between Luther and the papacy so much more than a theological dispute was the way in which Luther thought through the implications of his ideas in the three years between the *Ninety-five Theses* and the Bull *Exsurge Domine*. In the process he became a complete evangelical, in that the only authority he would accept for a religious belief or practice was the Bible. This led him to reject the Pope's claim of being God's appointed viceroy on earth, entrusted with the keys of heaven and hell, as no justification for it could be found in scripture. The whole structure of authority within the Church was therefore, in Luther's eyes, invalid as it was entirely based on this premise. It followed logically that neither the Pope nor anybody whose authority sprang from him had any right to pass judgement on Luther's ideas. It was for this reason that, when the Bull *Exsurge Domine* was burned publicly, the books of Canon Law, which defined the legal powers and practices of the Church, were also consigned to the flames. Luther was making clear his rejection of any authority that could not be justified in his interpretation of the Bible.

5 Frederick the Wise

> **KEY ISSUES** What was the significance of Frederick's decision to protect Luther? What were his motives for acting as he did?

Luther was not the first theologian in western Europe to take up this revolutionary position. But he was the first who was able both to maintain it and to avoid being put to death as a heretic. Others before him had either retracted or been killed. Why did this not happen to Luther?

The reasons were entirely political. Luther lived in the German state of Saxony where the Pope's direct influence was minimal. He was therefore compelled to work through the ruler, the Elector, Frederick the Wise. But Frederick was sympathetic to Luther from the outset, and Leo X, who wished to retain Frederick's support in the complex political manoeuvrings he was undertaking in Germany, was unwilling to risk alienating him. He preferred to wait until Luther had been given every opportunity to recant (withdraw his heretical statements). If persuasion failed he could then call upon Frederick to do his duty as a Christian prince. Hence the efforts made to persuade Luther that he was wrong to challenge the authority of the Church. But Frederick did not turn out to be as pliant as Leo had hoped. He was not prepared to be manipulated by him. It is the orthodox view of historians that without Frederick's protection Luther would have been executed as a heretic early in his career as a reformer. Yet it is not fully clear why the Elector acted as he did, eventually risking the anger of all who had the right and the power to act against him. It was not that he came under the personal influence of Luther. He was careful to keep a distance between them so that he could always claim that he had not met the man whom he was defending. It was therefore impossible for his opponents to claim that he had been bewitched. At first his motivation seems to have been purely political. Luther's attacks on Tetzel were in effect attacks on Albert of Brandenburg. The rivalry between Albert's and Frederick's families for influence in Germany was intense, so it was only natural that Frederick should defend one of his subjects who was attacking his enemy.

This motivation was quickly swallowed up in feelings of German nationalism. For many years there had been widespread resentment in Germany that the papacy had been able to extract huge quantities of money from the country in a way that was not possible in Spain or France or England. Luther tapped this reservoir of anti-papal feeling. His criticisms of the Pope were couched in nationalistic terms from the outset, and a large amount of the popular support he built up so rapidly was the result of his appeal to a common hatred of the grasping foreigner. Frederick shared these sentiments. When Luther was summoned to Rome by Pope Leo he was able to refuse because Frederick was firmly behind him and argued that any case against Luther should be heard on German soil. Even when the Bull *Exsurge Domine* was issued against Luther, Frederick chose to defend himself against the charge of failing to obey it by claiming that it carried no weight until Luther had had an opportunity to answer his accusers in person and in Germany.

Yet there was more to Frederick's support of Luther than these 'political' issues. Although he was not an early convert to the new religious beliefs, he was sufficiently interested and in touch with what Luther was teaching to understand that something of major importance was taking place in his small capital city. He was not prepared to stop it or to allow others to stop it until the rightness or wrongness of Luther's claims had been fairly decided. This meant approaching the issue with an open mind, and not doing as the Church authorities were so obviously doing - assuming that Luther was guilty of heresy and then searching for evidence to justify the assumption. In his dealings with the problem of what to do about Luther, Frederick seems to have started by acting in what he saw to be his own best interests. Within a short time, however, it appears that his determination to see 'fair play' and his developing feeling that Luther was probably right took over as the prime motivating forces that led him to make certain that Luther remained safe despite the storm that was gathering against him (see also pages 84-6 for Frederick's role after 1521).

6 The Diet of Worms

KEY ISSUES To what extent was the Diet of Worms a victory for the Pope? To what extent was it a victory for Luther?

Frederick was not, of course, a fully sovereign prince. He owed allegiance to the Holy Roman Emperor, as did the rulers of all the states in Germany. It was to the Emperor, sitting at a Diet (roughly equivalent to a parliament) attended by the princes and the representatives of the Imperial Cities, that unresolved issues of dispute were referred. Both Frederick and Pope Leo saw the Emperor as the most appropriate person to hear the case against Luther, given that it was obvious that popular opinion in Germany would not support any verdict that came from abroad. Leo, in particular, looked to the Emperor to provide moral and material support. His hopes were based on the knowledge that the newly elected Emperor, Charles V, although very young and inexperienced, was an ardent Catholic who took very seriously his responsibility of upholding the interests of the Church of Rome.

Charles became Emperor in 1519 while still a teenager. He was already the King of Spain and the ruler of the Burgundian provinces, including the Netherlands. He was potentially the most powerful European monarch since Charlemagne, seven centuries earlier. He arrived in Germany in time for a Diet that was to take place in the city

Martin Luther as a monk, by Lucas Cranach, 1520.

of Worms in April 1521. The Church authorities hoped that they would be able to secure the condemnation of Luther without him being given a hearing. They contended that his publications were by now so numerous and so clearly heretical that no defence was possible. But Charles was persuaded that it would be sensible to allow Luther to make an appearance so that there could be no complaint of unfair treatment. He was summoned to appear at Worms and was promised a safe conduct which would protect him from arrest whatever the outcome of his hearing.

His closest associates advised him not to appear. It was well known that, according to the Church's teaching, there was no need to keep one's promises to a heretic. It was also remembered that John Huss had been arrested and executed while under a safe conduct. But to Luther the likelihood of being killed was of no great concern. He regarded himself as being in God's hands, and was sure that if God meant him to live he would return safely from Worms. One thing he was certain of was that God wished him to preach the true gospel as widely as possible. So he travelled to Worms.

Even now the Pope's representatives hoped to limit Luther's participation to answering two questions - whether the books and pamphlets that had appeared in his name were really his, and whether he was prepared to abandon the views contained in them. But Luther out-manoeuvred them. He asked to be allowed to consider the questions overnight. His request was granted. On the next morning he answered 'Yes' to the first question, and set about explaining why the second question could not be properly answered in one word. He needed to differentiate between the different types of statements he had made. As he differentiated, he presented a clear summary of his position. Some of his writings expounded doctrine of which even the Pope approved. It would be wicked to disavow them. He had published writings

1 of another kind which inveigh against the papacy and the goings on of the papists. These books assail them as men who both by their doctrines as well as the disgraceful example of their lives have utterly laid waste the Christian world with evil both of the spirit and the flesh.

5 This fact none can deny or conceal. The experience of everybody and the complaints of the whole world bear witness that through the decrees of the Pope and the all too human doctrines of men the consciences of the faithful have been most wretchedly ensnared, harassed and butchered. Further, property and possessions, especially

10 in this illustrious land of Germany, have been devoured by an unbelievable tyranny, and are being devoured unceasingly in a most shocking manner ... If I retract these writings, it would be tantamount to supplying strength to this tyranny, and to opening not only windows but even doors to such great godlessness.

15 There is a third kind of book which I have written against certain

private, and as they call them, distinguished individuals. These are they who endeavour to maintain the Roman tyranny and to destroy the piety taught by me. Against these I confess I have been more severe than befits my religion or my profession. But then I do not set myself up as
20 a saint. It is not my life I am arguing about, but the teaching of Christ. It is not right for me to retract these works, because this very retraction would again bring about a state of affairs where tyranny and impiety would rule and rage among the people of God more violently than they ever ruled before.
25   However, because I am a man and not God, I cannot bring to bear any other protection for my books than my Lord Jesus Christ offered in respect of His teaching … Therefore I beg by the mercy of God that your most serene Majesty, most illustrious lordships, or any one at all, whether of high or low estate, who is competent, should bear witness,
30 expose my errors, overthrow me by the writings of the prophets and evangelists. I am more than ready, if the case be proven, to renounce every error no matter what it is. I shall be the first to consign my books to the flames.

Equally clear was the Church's case against him, which had remained constant throughout and had become stronger as Luther provided more and more evidence of his heretical thinking.

1 Is it not the case that you want Holy Scripture to be understood by your whim and your ideas? … Is it right to open to question and drag into dispute, those matters which the Catholic Church has judiciously settled, matters which have turned upon the usage, the rights and the
5 observances which our fathers held with absolute faith, for which there was no punishment, no torment they would not have undergone, indeed they would rather have endured a thousand deaths than have deviated from them a hair's breadth? Are you asking us to turn aside from the path which our fathers faithfully trod? … Do not, I entreat
10 you, Martin, do not arrogate to yourself that you, I repeat, that you are the one and only person who has knowledge of the Scriptures, who alone grasps the true sense of Holy Scripture … Do not make your judgement superior to that of so many of the most brilliant men. Do not seem to be wiser than all others. Do not cast doubt upon the most
15 holy orthodox faith, which Christ, the perfect lawgiver, instituted.

It was, of course, the political implications of Luther's stance that were uppermost in the minds of many of his opponents.

1 He despises the authority of the Church Fathers, an authority the Church accepts. He utterly takes away obedience and authority, and writes nothing which does not have the effect of promoting sedition, discord, war, murder, robbery and arson, and which does not subserve
5 the complete collapse of the Christian faith. He teaches a loose, self-willed kind of life, without any kind of law, utterly brutish. He himself is

a loose, self-willed person who condemns and suppresses all laws. This is shown when he burned in public the decretals and canon law, without fear and without shame. As he shows as much regard for the secular
10 sword as he does for the Pope's excommunication and its penalties, so has he done greater harm to secular law and order.

Given the evidence, there could be only one outcome to Luther's trial at Worms. He was found guilty of heresy. What was in doubt was the action that Charles would take as a result of this finding. To the horror of Frederick and the few other princes who sympathised with Luther's cause, the Emperor refused to consider a compromise solution. He was determined that Luther and all who supported him should be punished unless they immediately agreed to accept the teachings and authority of the Church. The Edict of Worms, which gave the decision legal force, confirmed that the terms of the Bull *Exsurge Domine* should be implemented; forbad any citizen of the Empire to provide Luther or his supporters with food or shelter, under pain of imprisonment and loss of property; and instructed all in authority within the Empire to search out and burn Luther's writings. The Pope had gained all he sought except Luther's detention.

By this time Luther had already left Worms, having been persuaded by powerful supporters that there was nothing to be gained by remaining and much to be lost if some enthusiast decided to take the law into his own hands. His 'escape' from Worms was well planned, as was his subsequent disappearance. As he and his escort were passing through a forest on their way to Wittenberg, they were seized by a group of unidentified horsemen who then rode off with Luther as their 'captive'. Frederick had decided that the political situation was too uncertain for the 'notorious heretic' to be anywhere but in hiding.

Working on Chapter 2

Now you need to work your way through the chapter for a second time, making notes as you go. There are two obvious approaches to use. It is for you to choose the approach which you think you can manage most successfully.

The most straightforward approach is to use the six key events as your main headings. Under each heading, using the sub-heading 'What happened', briefly describe in your own words the key features of the event. Then, add two further subsections about each event. For the first use the sub-heading 'Significance/Importance'. Your aim with these subsections should be to explain what part each event played in Luther's journey towards open defiance of the Pope. The second subsection will require you to do more thinking and to gather information from different parts of the chapter. Using the sub-heading 'Motives', try to explain briefly why each side acted as it did on each occasion. You will find that section 4 contains vital information about Luther's motives.

The second approach requires you to think for yourself throughout, which is more demanding but which is definitely better for you if you are able to do it. Use the chapter's six section headings as your main headings. Under each heading copy down the question or questions from the issues box. Then, in your own words, write down the key points you would use in answering the question. Make certain you include factual information to back up the general points you make. If you answer each question directly it is certain you will have thought through all the important issues the chapter covers, and it is likely you will have gained maximum benefit from the work you have done.

Summary Diagram
Luther's Revolt, 1517-21

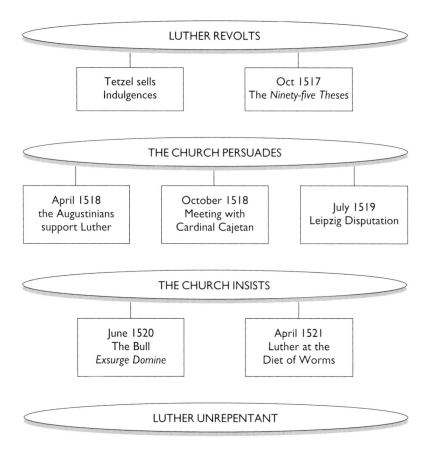

LUTHER REVOLTS

| Tetzel sells Indulgences | Oct 1517 The *Ninety-five Theses* |

THE CHURCH PERSUADES

| April 1518 the Augustinians support Luther | October 1518 Meeting with Cardinal Cajetan | July 1519 Leipzig Disputation |

THE CHURCH INSISTS

| June 1520 The Bull *Exsurge Domine* | April 1521 Luther at the Diet of Worms |

LUTHER UNREPENTANT

Answering structured and essay questions on Chapter 2

If the examination you are preparing to sit requires you to show your skills in extended writing by answering structured questions, you need to ensure you know a wide range of factual information about the key events covered by this chapter. It is not sufficient just to know about what happened, you also need to be able to put forward a clear point of view about why each event occurred and what were its main results/consequences. These are the '3 "c"s' (causes, course and consequences) described at the beginning of Chapter 1. As always, it is vital that you read the questions set very carefully in order to identify exactly what you are being asked to do.

Look at the following two questions:

1a) Explain what the Pope hoped to achieve in his dealings with Luther between 1518 and 1521?
  b) How successful was he in achieving what he intended?
  c) Why was he not more successful?
2a) Outline the stages by which, between 1517 and 1521, Martin Luther came into conflict with the Catholic Church.
  b) Why did Luther take the action he did?

In an examination situation it might be very tempting to answer the first part of question **2** by writing down all you know about what Martin Luther did, 1517-21. However, doing so would not gain you all the available marks. Only if you select from the facts you know to answer the question directly are you likely to score highly. It would be good practice to write an answer to this question. It would provide you with useful experience in distinguishing between relevant and irrelevant knowledge.

Those who will be answering full essay questions in their examination will normally be faced with questions which require knowledge and understanding of the whole of Luther's life. However, they will sometimes come across questions which concentrate on the period 1517-21. Such questions tend to focus on one of three topics:

1. the issues over which Luther fell out with the Church;
2. the strategy, if any, followed by Luther in his 'revolt'; and,
3. the reasons for Luther's early success in building up support.

Source-based questions on Chapter 2

1. The sale of Indulgences, 1517

Read the extracts from Luther's letter to the Archbishop of Mainz on page 25, and from the *Ninety-five Theses* on page 27. Study the illustration on page 26. Answer the following questions:

a) In what way did Luther attempt to put pressure on the Archbishop?
(4 marks)

b) Using evidence from the illustration and from the extracts, describe the sales techniques used by John Tetzel. *(6 marks)*

c) Using evidence from both extracts, explain Luther's objections to Tetzel's sale of indulgences. *(6 marks)*

d) Was the artist who produced the illustration sympathetic or hostile to Tetzel? Explain your answer. *(4 marks)*

2. *Luther at the Diet of Worms, 1521*

Read the extracts from the reports on what took place at the Diet, given on pages 34-6. Answer the following questions:

a) In the first extract, what argument does Luther use to justify his refusal to retract his writings? What does he imply is a possible way forward? *(3 marks)*

b) Explain the argument used, in the second extract, to try to persuade Luther to retract his writings. *(3 marks)*

c) In what ways did Luther, in the first extract, and his opponents, in the third extract, attempt to appeal to the fears and prejudices of their audience? *(6 marks)*

d) What do the extracts suggest was Luther's status at the Diet? Give evidence to support your answer. *(5 marks)*

3. *Portraits of Luther*

Study the portraits of Luther reproduced on pages 33, 46 and 69, and answer the following questions:

a) What were the likely motives of the two artists in producing their portraits? Explain your answer. *(5 marks)*

b) How useful are the portraits in helping to decide what Luther actually looked like? *(5 marks)*

c) Which portrait is likely to be the more accurate? Why? *(5 marks)*

d) What approximate date would you assign to the illustration reproduced on page 46? Explain your answer. *(5 marks)*

When answering source-based questions it is often difficult to think of enough points to make to stand a reasonable chance of gaining all the marks allocated. For example, you are likely to find this a problem when answering the four parts of question **3**. In these circumstances it is usually worth spending a couple of minutes trying to think of something else relevant to say. The one or two additional marks this might gain you could easily affect your final grade. It would be good experience for you to attempt written answers to question **3** in which you try hard to make enough points to earn five marks for each part.

3 Luther's Teachings

POINTS TO CONSIDER

Luther believed in a small number of theological issues fervently. To him they were matters of life and death. As you read this chapter identify what these issues were and what Luther's beliefs about them were. Other issues concerned him less and he made little effort to publicise his opinions about them until the situation forced him to do so. In the meantime, his views were often misrepresented, sometimes with horrendous results. You need to identify where this happened and to reach your own conclusions about how far Luther was to blame for what he did or did not do.

KEY DATES

1520 Publication of 'On the Babylonish Captivity of the Church', 'The Address to the German Nobility', and 'Of the Liberty of the Christian Man'.
1522 Luther's translation of the New Testament published.
1523 Imperial Knights defeated.
1525 Peasants' Revolt; *Against the Robbing and Murdering Hordes of Peasants* published.
1526 Luther's translation of the Mass published.
1529 'Large Catechism' and 'Small Catechism' published.
1534 Luther's translation of the Old Testament published.
1540 Philip of Hesse bigamy scandal.

Three-and-a-half years had elapsed between Luther's initial challenge to the Church's beliefs and practices and his condemnation at the Diet of Worms. During this time he had changed from being an unknown Saxon university professor to being a German national hero and a theologian with an international reputation. There was hardly anyone of learning or social position in western Europe who had not heard of him. He was variously hated as the disturber of the *status quo* who was likely to stimulate a social as well as a religious revolution by his attacks on established authority, and idolised as the latter-day prophet who would right the wrongs of the world. Hopes and fears of him were equally exaggerated. The Pope's representatives at the Diet of Worms were convinced that the whole of Germany was about to fall under Luther's spell unless drastic action was taken, while many of the poor were convinced that somehow he would bring an end to their exploitation. What had happened to create these contrary views and expectations?

Luther had been immensely busy since the *Ninety-five Theses* had brought him to public notice. He had continued to study the Bible in detail and to think through the implications of his earlier conviction that salvation comes from faith alone (see page 30). As his understanding of what he was sure was the real meaning of the Bible grew, he not only preached 'the truth' in Wittenberg but also wrote an enormous number of tracts which were printed and widely circulated. Never before had so much appeared in print from the pen of one man. The variety was remarkable. There were serious academic works in Latin, closely argued justifications of his position in German, and what were essentially pieces of propaganda attacking the Pope in highly abusive terms, aimed at the common people. Given that the technology of the time meant that every page of every copy had to be printed separately and laboriously, the output from the presses was colossal. Between 1517 and 1520 about 300 000 copies of his various works were printed. But supply could not meet demand, such was the interest created by Luther. Copies of his works were passed from hand to hand. They were eagerly read or listened to throughout Germany, and especially in the towns and cities, where most of the literate population lived. Very few people in the countryside could read.

1 The Publications of 1520

> **KEY ISSUES** What were Luther's motives in producing each of his three main publications of 1520? How did the publications' contents illustrate these motives?

a) On the Babylonish Captivity of the Church

By 1520 many of Luther's ideas were well developed. During that year he wrote 24 works for publication, including the three that are generally thought to encapsulate his teaching during the early stages of his career as a reformer. The most theologically significant was, *On the Babylonish Captivity of the Church*. The title was an attempt to link the Pope's rule of the Church with the Old Testament story of the Israelites being taken as slaves to Babylon. It was written in Latin and was intended for an academic audience. In it Luther argued that Christianity had been captured and enslaved by the papacy with beliefs and practices that were man-made rather than springing from the word of God. At the heart of Catholicism were the seven sacraments (sacred religious ceremonies), which could only be carried out by priests, and which were claimed to be the vital channels of communication between God and humanity. Thus nobody could be saved without the services of the Church, administered by priests.

Luther refused to accept that there were seven sacraments. He argued that something could only be a sacrament if it were both uniquely Christian and had been established by Jesus. Only two of the seven matched these criteria. Both baptism and the sharing of bread and wine (the Catholic Eucharist, celebrated during the mass) were clearly justified by the New Testament. The other five, as taught by the Church, were invalid. The fact that he denied the sacramental nature of confirmation (by which older children were allowed entry to the adult congregation), matrimony (marriage) and extreme unction (by which the dying were cleansed of their sins) was of no great significance in practice because there were few implications flowing from the changed status of these rites. Much more serious was Luther's denial of penance and ordination as sacraments.

The sacrament of penance was used by the Church to ensure that people generally behaved in a moral and law-abiding manner. The Church claimed that through this sacrament it was able to forgive sins on God's behalf, and that, by refusing the sacrament to an individual, it was able to condemn him to eternal damnation. Luther strongly contested this claim. He argued that the forgiveness of sins was a private matter between the believer and God, in which the priest did not have a vital part to play. If Luther's contention was correct, it would be impossible for the priests to exercise their customary role as the dispensers of pardons, for which they could make charges. It was not that Luther was advocating the abolition of confession and subsequent absolution (telling people that their sins were forgiven): he was merely drawing attention to the fact that it was God who forgave sins. The priest's role was only to confirm that this had happened.

The sacrament of orders (ordination) by which a man became a priest was at the heart of the structure of the Catholic Church. It was the justification for treating priests as an elite group who were separate from and above ordinary people. As the only ones able to make direct contact with God they were to be especially valued and respected. They could not be subjected to the legal requirements that applied to other citizens or subjects. The special rights and exemptions that priesthood conferred was the cause of much of the hatred of churchmen that was so prevalent in Germany. Luther was convinced that it was justified:

1   Of this sacrament the Church of Christ knows nothing: it was invented by the Church of the Pope. It not only has no promise of grace, anywhere declared, but not a word is said about it in the whole of the New Testament. Now it is ridiculous to set up as a Sacrament of God
5   that which can nowhere be proved to have been instituted by God. ... Let every man who has learnt that he is a Christian recognise what he is, and be certain that we are all equally priests, that is that we have the same power in the word, and in any sacrament whatever, although it is not lawful for anyone to use this power, except with the consent of the
10 community.

His claim that priests were no different to other people, except that they had been authorised by their community to carry out certain functions, was a repetition of the doctrine of 'the priesthood of all believers', that he had formulated earlier in the year.

b) The Address to the German Nobility

This revolutionary doctrine underpinned the whole of his treatise, *To the Christian Nobility of the German Nation Respecting the Reformation of the Christian Estate*, often known as *The Address to the German Nobility*. This pamphlet was written in German and, as its name implies, was directed at the lay rulers of Germany. Its central argument was that successive Popes had perverted the true Christianity, and that, because the present Pope had refused to correct the abuses that had been clearly drawn to his attention, the responsibility for doing so now fell upon those to whom God had given power in secular matters. He countered the traditional defence of the Pope, that nobody but him was empowered to take action in spiritual matters, both by dismissing the Pope's claim to primacy within the Church, and by challenging the assumption that the clergy formed a separate elite group with special powers:

1 It is a wickedly devised fable - and they cannot quote a single letter to confirm it - that it is for the Pope alone to interpret the scriptures or to confirm interpretations of them. They have assumed the authority of their own selves. And though they say that this authority was given to
5 St Peter when the keys were given to him, it is plain enough that the keys were not given to St Peter alone, but to the whole community ...
    It has been devised that the Pope, bishops, priests and monks are called the spiritual estate; princes, lords, artificers and peasants are the temporal estate. This is an artful lie and hypocritical device, but let no
10 one be made afraid by it, and that for this reason: that all Christians are truly of the spiritual estate, and there is no difference among them, save of office alone ... Thus we are all consecrated as priests by baptism ...

Thus Luther was arguing not only in favour of 'the priesthood of all believers', but also for a reversal of the traditional relationship between Church and state. For many centuries the papacy had claimed, often with success, that all secular authorities, from emperors and kings downwards, were under the general control of the Church, and that the intervention of the Church in secular matters was justified in extreme situations, whereas it was forbidden for laymen to interfere in spiritual matters. By dismissing the concept of a separate spiritual domain, Luther was inviting the lay rulers of Germany to assume control of religious affairs within their territories. He had clearly abandoned all hope of reforming the Church from within. It would be necessary to impose change from outside. This idea, more than any other put forward by Luther, was to mark the end of the medieval concept of Christendom, and to usher in the modern secular age.

c) Of the Liberty of the Christian Man

The third of the important writings of 1520 was, *Of the Liberty of the Christian Man*. In it Luther further developed the implications of his belief in 'justification by faith alone'. He was eager to counter the argument that, if salvation is to be gained merely by believing in God, it does not matter what one does and how many sins one commits. He knew that many people were already interpreting him as meaning this, and that this was likely to discredit him in the eyes of the morally-minded majority. He therefore attempted to clarify his teachings on 'good works':

1   As Christ says, 'A good tree cannot bring forth evil fruit, neither can a
    corrupt tree bring forth good fruit'. Now it is clear that the fruit does
    not bear the tree, nor does the tree grow on the fruit; but, on the
    contrary, the trees bear the fruit, and the fruit grows on the trees.
5   As then the trees must exist before the fruit, and as the fruit does
    not make the tree either good or bad, but, on the contrary, a tree of
    either kind produces fruit of the same kind, so must first the person of
    the man be good or bad before he can do either a good or a bad work;
    and his works do not make him bad or good, but he himself makes his
10 works either bad or good ...
        We do not then reject good works; nay, we embrace them and teach
    them in the highest degree. It is not on their own account that we
    condemn them, but on account of this impious addition to them and the
    perverse notion of seeking justification by them.

2 Religious Practices

> **KEY ISSUES** What were the main changes in religious practices introduced in Lutheran churches? Which of these changes did Luther personally support?

Luther adopted the same approach when considering religious practices. While some of his leading followers were becoming very worked up over issues such as paintings and images in churches, the vestments of priests (the clothes they wore during services), the continuation of monasteries, clerical celibacy (priests not being allowed to marry), confessing and fasting, Luther maintained the view that these were matters of peripheral importance. They did not greatly interest him, and certainly were not matters of life and death to him, as were 'justification by faith alone', 'the priesthood of all believers', and his understanding of the purpose and nature of the Mass.

But they were matters that could not be ignored, if only because others considered them to be of importance, and were prepared to cause trouble over them. He therefore had to take up a position in relation to these issues. His policy was that if the Bible did not forbid an activity, it should only be discontinued if common sense suggested that this was preferable to its continuation. So he was prepared to see churches cleansed of paintings and images if the community considered them to be a distraction from listening to the word of God; priests conducting services in everyday clothes if expensive vestments were thought to mark them out as being more important than they really were; monasteries closed if it was agreed that their incomes could be put to better uses; priests marrying if this removed them from sexual temptation; confession discontinued if it smacked too much of priestly intervention in the relationship between the believer and God; and the rules of fasting broken if to continue with them was to cause unnecessary hardship.

In practice, all these things happened in areas that became Lutheran. Luther was even prepared to encourage some of them himself. He could see that there was no justification for allowing monasteries to continue once he had rejected the Catholic teaching that the taking of vows and the living of life according to them conferred automatic salvation. He wanted to see the incomes of the monasteries put to good use in providing food for the poor and education for the young. In England the lands of the dissolved monasteries went to the king and the wealthy landed classes: in the areas of Germany that became Lutheran, the property of the monastic houses was either returned to the original benefactors, if still living, or retained by the community for charitable purposes.

There was, of course, the problem of what to do with the men and women who had renounced their vows and returned to the world. As Luther taught that all work was equally valuable in the eyes of God, there was no doctrinal difficulty in allowing the men to take up whatever occupation best suited their skills and experience. For the women it was not so easy. Many nuns came from wealthy families, because only they were able to make the size of donation that was normally demanded before a girl was admitted to a nunnery. Few jobs were open to women besides domestic and agricultural service, and these were inappropriate for people of any breeding. The only alternative was marriage or a return to their families. Strenuous efforts were made to find suitable husbands for as many of the younger ex-nuns as possible.

In 1523 nine nuns who wished to renounce their vows were smuggled out of ducal Saxony, which was still Catholic, and brought to Wittenberg. Husbands were eventually found for all but one. The remaining ex-nun, Katherine von Bora, kept reminding Luther of his promise to find her a husband so that she could leave the domestic service into which she had been placed. After two years and with no suitable husband in sight, Luther thought that he ought to offer to marry her himself. She accepted, and the Luther household became a focal point for the Reformation in Germany. Katherine coped extremely well with a never-ending stream of visitors and resident students, while bearing and bringing up six children, and coping with a man who rarely seemed to stop working for long enough to be more than passing company.

So, somewhat fortuitously because he had intended never to marry, Luther was able to put into practice his teachings about marriage. He regarded a person's duty to spouse, children and parents as second in importance only to one's duty to God. Thus, family life, and the relationships within it, was at the very heart of the practice of Lutheranism. It was for this reason that Luther was prepared actively to encourage priests to marry, so that they could set a good example to their congregations. He had expected not to do so himself because he was already a middle-aged man in his forties (beyond the generally accepted age for marriage) whose future was anything but secure. But, in the event, he was able to share in a marriage of over 20 years that, by all accounts, was just of the type he advocated.

By the time Luther was married, the churches in Wittenberg had been cleared of their embellishments. But he was not prepared to see worship stripped of all its colour. He had a passion for music, which he regarded as one of God's most precious gifts to humanity, and he was determined that its role in church services should be enhanced

Luther and Katherine von Bora.

rather than diminished. This would be done in part by encouraging the new element of corporate hymn-singing. To facilitate this, Luther wrote and published over 20 hymns, and others soon followed his example. He was also keen that choirs should be retained in churches, and he prepared suitable words and music for them to sing.

Luther found it impossible totally to separate worship and education in his mind. He saw the task of the Church as much in terms of instructing its congregation in the word of God as of offering Him praise. Hymns were for worship, but they were also intended as easily memorable statements of belief. But much more important than hymns was the Bible. He knew that the most important educational task confronting the Church was to bring the New Testament, in particular, to as many people as possible.

3 The Bible

> **KEY ISSUE** In what ways did Luther's ideas about the Bible differ from those that were traditional in the Catholic Church?

In traditional Catholic worship the Bible was of very little importance. A few key passages were incorporated in services, but they were read in Latin, which was sometimes not even understood by the priest. There was no attempt made to ensure that the congregation knew what the words meant. This was not thought odd by most people, as the congregation's main function was to witness the service, not to partake in it. Nor was it thought appropriate for lay people to study the Bible, as they would in all probability misunderstand it. Lay people would be told what to believe. There was no need for them to read the Bible themselves.

Luther, of course, fundamentally disagreed with this view of the clergy as the mediators between God (and his word) and ordinary men and women. He believed that the role of the priest was to help each person to make direct contact with God. To do this, everybody should understand the Bible as fully as possible, which meant having it available in a language they could understand. There were at least 18 translations of the Bible into German in existence but Luther felt that they were all very inadequate as they contained many errors, as well as not conforming with his interpretation of several key passages. He therefore reached an early decision to make his own translation.

When Luther was seized as he was returning from the Diet of Worms (see page 36), he was taken to the Elector Frederick's remote castle of the Wartburg, where he surrendered his monk's habit and lived under the assumed name of Squire George. Only his closest associates knew of his whereabouts. But his time was not wasted. In only three months he translated the whole of the New Testament into German. It was printed and on sale by the end of 1522. Although he was never completely satisfied with it, and constantly revised it during the next 24 years, it was a great literary masterpiece. It was a relatively free translation in which Luther used the everyday German metaphors of the time - often described as 'earthy' - to make sure that ordinary people would understand the message in terms of their own experience. This was reinforced by numerous wood-cut illustrations which clearly placed the Bible stories in sixteenth-century Germany. The result was a book that rapidly became the benchmark for German language and literature, just as James I's Authorised Version became for English three generations later.

The translation of the Old Testament came to fruition more slowly as it was never again possible to find time as free from other responsibilities as were the seven months spent in the Wartburg. Publication was in 1534. Again the approach used was the same. Luther stated that one of his aims had been 'to make Moses so German that no one would suspect he was a Jew'. The result was a translation with which the people of Germany could identify. Hundreds of thousands of copies were produced during Luther's lifetime and they were to be found almost everywhere German was read or spoken. But producing the raw material for studying God's revelation was not sufficient. People needed considerable guidance in appreciating what lay behind the words.

4 Dissemination

> **KEY ISSUES** What methods did Luther use to disseminate his teachings? How successful was he in his dissemination?

Luther worked hard to ensure that his teachings reached as many people as possible. He was an untiring preacher, and he expected others with any ability to follow his example. Listening to sermons became almost the central religious activity in reformed congregations. Given the evangelical nature of Lutheranism, it is not surprising that most of the sermons were expositions of portions of the Bible, with clear indications of how their content should affect belief, religious practices and everyday behaviour. Luther's sermons were long (normally more than an hour) but his listeners do not seem to have found difficulty in this. This is perhaps hard for us to understand, conditioned as we are by the media to much shorter spans of concentration, but the clues are to be found in the texts of the more than 2300 of Luther's sermons that have survived. He talked to people at their level, using examples culled from their shared experience, while managing to illuminate the mysteries of life, its purpose, and its relationship to God. He was meeting a need that many people felt. Many of his sermons were published and were sold in large numbers.

But Luther and his sermons could not be everywhere. As more and more of Germany became Lutheran there was an obvious need for a clear statement of the central beliefs of the reformed religion so that families and local groups, which were perhaps without an educated pastor, could teach both the young and the old effectively. Luther supplied this in 1529 when his *Large Catechism,* aimed at adults, and his *Small Catechism,* for use with children, were published. These catechisms were intended to be read regularly by each believer, with the most important sections being memorised. It became a normal procedure in Lutheran households for the father to test his family on the catechism every Sunday. Once again Luther had shown his skill and vision in communicating his message. Never before had there been such a carefully thought-out and structured method of ensuring the religious instruction of children. The catechisms were used both in churches and in homes. Luther had hoped that they would also be much in evidence in schools, but he was disappointed. He was generally unable to convince others that the establishment of schools was a high priority, and he was to continue to complain for the rest of his life about the very small percentage of German children who attended school. It seemed to him that unless something more was done there would be no hope of providing an educated pastor for each congregation. He was right, but it was not until after his death that the issue was seriously tackled.

Luther cared greatly about education, which he viewed totally in terms of religion, but he cared even more about the correctness of the beliefs that were to be taught. Like other Christian religious thinkers of his age, he was certain that God had revealed Himself to humanity through the life of Jesus Christ. And in common with all evangelical reformers, he was convinced that the Bible contained this revelation in its entirety. As it appeared self-evident to him that God would know what He meant, and would have only one message on any one point, he had no doubt that there could be no more than one correct interpretation of any passage of scripture. Therefore a theological point of view was either right or wrong - there was no middle position. And if an interpretation was wrong, it must be the work of the Devil. As such it was likely to bring innocent people into mortal sin, thus causing their eternal damnation. It was for this reason that he was prepared to reflect on the exact meaning of a phrase in scripture *ad nauseam,* and to dispute minor differences of interpretation to lengths and with amounts of aggression and hostility that defy normal reason.

5 The Eucharist

KEY ISSUES What were Luther's beliefs about the Eucharist? Why did many of his followers find these beliefs hard to accept?

The issue Luther felt most strongly about was the celebration that was at the heart of Catholic worship, the Eucharist. It was based on the Last Supper Jesus shared with his disciples on the evening before he was crucified, as described in the New Testament. Theologians had created a complex pattern of beliefs around it. The Church's teaching was that during the service a literal re-enaction of Christ's death occurred when, at the moment the officiating priest offered the dedication, the bread and wine on the altar turned into the actual body and blood of Jesus. This doctrine of transubstantiation depended on a belief that Jesus was speaking literally in using the words 'This is my blood' and 'This is my body' when describing the wine and the bread during the Last Supper. It was taught that transubstantiation was a 'great mystery', inexplicable in rational terms, but none-the-less true. Every priest, however personally sinful, had the ability to perform this miracle, and to cause Christ to suffer death once again. To eat the body of Christ at the mass was seen as being of great merit, conferring on the participants a degree of grace which offset some of their sins in the eyes of God. It was even believed that this grace could extend to the dead who were suffering in purgatory, and that masses performed in their names would shorten the time they had to suffer before entering heaven. Many wealthy people had left money in their wills for the employment of priests, known as chantry priests, whose only responsibility was to perform a set number of masses each day in their benefactor's name.

Luther came to the conclusion early on that to regard the Eucharist as a sacrifice and as a vehicle of grace was a perversion of God's purpose. It followed from 'justification by faith alone' that participation in masses could not confer merit in the way that the Church taught. This did not mean that he considered the mass to be unimportant. He was emotionally very committed to it, for its celebration had provided him with some of his deepest spiritual experiences, and he was determined that it should continue to play a leading part in the pattern of worship. He wished to retain the service much as he had experienced it since childhood. But his colleagues persuaded him that two significant changes should be made.

The mass was spoken in Latin, and few in the congregation could understand what was being said. Luther's conservative inclination was to retain the use of Latin, while removing references to the sacrificial nature of the sacrament, which is what he did initially. However it did not take long to convince him that it was indefensible for the service not to be in the vernacular (native language). In 1526 his German version of the mass was published. Nor did it take him long to accept that the practice of offering the congregation only the bread during mass should be discontinued. It had been justified on the grounds that it would be sacrilege for any of the blood of Christ to be spilled, and that if the cup were to be offered to the congregation this would probably happen. So the cup was drunk from only by the priest, while all partook of the bread. The change to offering the Eucharist to the congregation in both kinds, i.e. both the bread and the wine, became a hallmark of reformed practices, and was often the first thing to be done as a community moved away from Catholicism.

Despite the changes that he initiated or was prepared to allow, Luther soon found himself accused of being a papist at heart as far as the Eucharist was concerned. Many of his own supporters felt that he was remaining too close to both the theory and the practice of the Catholic mass. In terms of the practice, about which he had personal preferences rather than theological certainty, he was content to countenance a variety of procedures as suited the wishes of each congregation. But many of the previous practices remained, and it became customary for Lutheran churches to continue with the elaborate ceremonial that many later Protestants found offensive, although he could see good sense in changing the name of the mass to 'the Holy Communion' or 'the Lord's Supper'. Yet he was ferocious in maintaining the detail of the theological beliefs that lay behind his conception of the service. Those who disagreed with him were gently corrected at first. If they did not accept their correction they were likely to find themselves attacked in print as agents of the Devil. Luther lost many potential adherents because he was unmoving over the theology of the Eucharist.

The question at issue was the exact nature of Christ's presence during the service. The Catholic doctrine of transubstantiation depended on a philosophical acceptance that there were two aspects to the reality of objects. These were the 'accidents', the substance immediately apparent to our senses, and the 'essence', the intangible quality which marked out the identity of the object. For example, the 'accidents' of a table were wood, and its 'essence' was what made it different from a pile of wood, a stool or a chair. So, during the mass, it was the 'essence' of the bread and wine that turned into the flesh and blood of Jesus, while the 'accidents' remained unchanged.

Luther rejected transubstantiation and replaced it with what modern writers have termed consubstantiation, although the word was unknown in the sixteenth century. Consubstantiation involved the possibility of more than one 'element' being present in an object. 'Elements', according to the scientific thinking of the day, could be materials such as earth or water, or intangibles such as fire and wind. Luther explained his doctrine by using the analogy of iron being heated. He taught that just as the iron remains iron when the fire enters it and occupies every part, so the bread remains bread when it is entered by Jesus' body during Holy Communion. Thus he was at one with the Catholics in believing in the real presence of Jesus during the service.

Over this issue more than any other, Luther seemed to allow his own feelings to overcome his judgement. His long and increasingly desperate defences of his position have the air of someone attempting to rationalise a prejudice. It was not that he was a proud man who was unprepared to admit that he was wrong, or that he was unwilling to learn from others. One of his most endearing qualities, and one that helped to retain the loyalty of some very able followers, was his open-ness to correction and new ideas, as long as they did not come from anybody he considered to be under the influence of Satan. Over the theology of the Eucharist, however, he had struggled and prayed for so long that he was certain God had revealed its true meaning to him. This belief was bolstered by the immense personal spiritual comfort he received from feeling Jesus' real presence during Holy Communion. He came to hate anyone who argued that the service was merely symbolic, or that the presence was spiritual rather than substantial.

6 Politics and Society

> **KEY ISSUES** Why and with what results were Luther's ideas on political and social issues misunderstood? What evidence is there that his views were essentially conservative? In what ways did his conservative views assist the spread of Lutheranism?

Such strength of feeling was limited to matters that had to do with theology, and especially with theology that related to salvation. This was Luther's compelling interest and driving force. Other issues did not generally interest him, and it was with considerable reluctance that he devoted time to them. Apart from his love of music and his concern for religious-based education, he tended to venture into non-doctrinal matters only spasmodically, when his intervention seemed to be particularly called for. Otherwise he was content to allow those interested in social and political matters a fairly free rein. But he did establish very clear parameters within which they should operate.

In political and social matters Luther was essentially an instinctive conservative. He thought about them to no great depth, and was much influenced by the values and attitudes he had learned as a child. To these he added little as a result of his studies of the scrip-tures, which generally confirmed his existing views, except that he became convinced that earthly concerns were of little importance compared with spiritual matters. At the heart of his thinking was a deep respect for authority. Although he violently rejected the Pope's claim to authority over the Christian Church, he equally strongly championed the cause of authority in secular affairs. He believed that secular rulers, from the Emperor downwards, received their 'power of the sword' directly from God. They must therefore be obeyed in all earthly matters, even if their actions were tyrannous and unjust, for only God could remove powers He had bestowed. If secular rulers abused their God-given powers they would be answerable to Him in the life after death. In the meantime, it was the duty of all good Christians to abide by the laws and rules that they imposed.

Luther's views on political and social roles and responsibilities were unknown during his early years of prominence. But both his supporters and his enemies made assumptions about them. They incorrectly assumed that, because he was violently opposed to the traditional authority of the Pope, he was hostile to established authority in all its forms. This led the higher social orders generally to fear his influence, and those who wished to see alterations in the existing order of things generally to look upon him as a latter-day messiah who would lead them to victory in their struggle for radical change.

a) The Imperial Knights

The heyday of the Imperial Knights had been during the early middle ages, when their military services had been much valued by the Emperor. But by the early sixteenth century this class of minor nobles, whose members owed allegiance to the Emperor alone, had declined to relative insignificance. The Emperor was no longer acting as the policeman of Germany. This role had been taken over by local princes who had managed to establish for themselves a position of virtual independence. They resented the presence within their territories of the knights, many of whom owned a castle and controlled a sizeable body of soldiers, but did not recognise their authority. Numbers of the knights had come to terms with the reality of their situation and had entered the service of local rulers or had attached themselves to the Emperor's court in a non-military capacity. But many had not. These constituted a group of mercenary leaders, some followed by a mere handful of men, who tended to look upon the fragmentation of the Empire into numerous semi-independent states as the cause of their troubles. They therefore developed a primitive style of German nationalism based on a desire to see a consolidated Empire with strong central control and the elimination of foreign influence. The foreign domination they disliked most was that of the Pope. They also objected to the fact that the Church, through its bishops and archbishops, was the secular authority in roughly a fifth of Germany. They therefore viewed Luther, when he became a declared enemy of the papacy, as an important potential ally.

The knights were not a coherent or a co-ordinated political and military force. They came together as the need arose. Their leading personalities were Ulrich von Hutten and Franz von Sickingen. Hutten was that most rare of characters, a successful military man who was also a poet, philosopher and publicist of note. Before the emergence of Luther he was already well known for his vitriolic attacks on the Pope for the way he milked Germany of money. Seeing the popular appeal that Luther could bring to the cause, Hutten persuaded Sickingen, the most outstanding of the knights' military leaders, that armed protection should be offered to the Wittenberg professor. Luther declined, not because he objected to support from this quarter, but because it was unnecessary while he retained the confidence of Frederick the Wise. But the knights provided a safe haven for numbers of reformers from other parts of Germany who wished to follow Luther's example but were forced to flee because their local ruler was hostile. More than this, they decided after the Diet of Worms in 1521 that the time was right to lead a popular crusade against the territorial power of the Church and in favour of the reformed religion of Luther. They began by launching an attack on the lands of the Archbishop of Trier in 1522. But they had misjudged the situation. Not only did the Archbishop not crumble before them, but in stoutly resisting he managed to win the active support of other local princes who were pleased to come together in an attempt to break the military power of the unruly knights once and for all. Sickingen was finally defeated in 1523 and the knights were destroyed as a significant political force. Sickingen fled to Switzerland and Hutten died of syphilis, the public health scourge of sixteenth century Europe. Although Luther had not been involved personally in the venture, the fact that the attack had been carried out partly in his name further convinced many people that Luther's ideas were synonymous with anarchy.

b) The Peasants' War

A potentially even more damaging situation came to a head in 1525. For more than a century peasant discontent had been widespread in Germany, erupting from time to time in bouts of violence against the sources of economic oppression, especially the Church and the landowners. It was not just that the peasants felt that too great a proportion of the fruits of their labours was going to others. They were outraged that this amount was being increased year by year as the owners of rights over them were attempting to maximise their incomes in the face of pressure from rising prices. In common with many other conservative peasantries in other places at other times, it was change rather than simple hardship that stimulated violent action in the German countryside. The increased financial demands coincided in the 1520s with the spread of new ideas. Much of the peasantry was deeply religious despite the economic demands made by the Church. The ideas of Luther, especially the stress laid on the Bible rather than on traditional dogma, were gladly received, although often in a perverted form which taught that the dues payable to the Church were unjustified and should be withheld. Added to this were the naive beliefs that the Emperor would redress their grievances if only he knew of them, and that Luther would come to lead them in their fight.

Numerous local uprisings in 1524 turned into a widespread general rising in 1525. Although given the name of the Peasants' War, and despite a common symbol (the *Bundschuh*, or peasant's shoe) and a common programme for the removal of financial impositions, the struggle was lacking in centralised planning or co-ordination. Local groups copied one another's programmes and activities, and sometimes came together for joint action, but concerted action was never taken to any real purpose. Hundreds of castles and religious houses were ransacked and towns were plundered, but there was rarely any attempt to replace the overthrown structures of authority with anything besides mob rule. It was therefore relatively easy for the princes to re-establish their control once the initial enthusiasm for revolt had subsided. This they did with large-scale reprisals, aimed at removing the potential leadership of future risings and frightening the remainder into submission. They were successful. It is probable that in the process upwards of 100 000 peasants were executed.

Hundreds of priests who had declared themselves to be followers of Luther marched and fought alongside the peasants, and many contemporaries and some modern Catholic historians have argued that Luther consciously encouraged the uprising. No evidence exists to substantiate this claim other than the circumstantial evidence of Luther expressing sympathy for the grievances of the peasants, and the indirect evidence of many of his followers joining the rebels. What seems more likely is that Luther was initially sympathetic to the plight of the peasants but was soon horrified by the excesses of their actions. Certainly, his reaction was equally extreme. He expressed his opinion in one of his most famous tracts, *Against the Robbing and Murdering Hordes of Peasants*, written while the rising was at its height. This tract clearly presented his views on political issues. He was adamant that the peasants 'have abundantly merited death in body and soul' by their actions. He specified three justifications for his verdict:

1 In the first place they have sworn to be true and faithful, submissive and obedient, to their rulers, as Christ commands, when he says, 'Render unto Caesar the things that are Caesar's', and 'Let everyone be subject unto the higher powers'. Because they are breaking this obedience, and
5 are setting themselves against the higher powers, wilfully and with violence, they have forfeited body and soul, as faithless, perjured, lying, disobedient knaves and scoundrels are wont to do ...
   In the second place, they are starting a rebellion, and violently robbing and plundering monasteries and castles which are not theirs ...
10 In the third place, they cloak this terrible and horrible sin with the Gospel ... and compel people to hold with them in these abominations. Thus they become the greatest of blasphemers of God and slanderers of his holy Name, serving the devil, under the outward appearance of the Gospel ... I have never heard of a more hideous sin.

He went on to advise the princes of what they should do in this situation:

1 First, I will not oppose a ruler who, even though he does not tolerate
the Gospel, will smite and punish these peasants without offering to
submit the case to judgement ... It is their duty to punish them, for it
is just for this purpose that they bear the sword, and are 'the ministers
5 of God upon him that doeth evil' ... For a prince and lord must
remember in this case that he is God's minister and the servant of his
wrath, to whom the sword is committed for use upon such fellows, and
that he sins as greatly against God, if he does not punish and protect
and does not fulfil the duties of his office, as does one to whom the
10 sword has not been committed when he commits a murder. If he can
punish and does not - even though the punishment consists in the taking
of life and the shedding of blood - then he is guilty of all the murder and
all the evil which these fellows commit ...

The rulers, then, should go on unconcerned, and with a good
15 conscience lay about them as long as their hearts still beat.

When this tract appeared from the printers the slaughter of the peasants was already in full swing. The timing of its publication made it
look as if Luther was callous and heartless. It was even claimed by his
opponents that he was a turncoat, deserting those he had formerly
encouraged once it was clear which was to be the winning side.
Although this was clearly unfair, there have been few attempts to
justify his advocacy of extreme vengeance and his urging of the
princes to 'stab, smite, slay, whoever can. If you die in doing it, well for
you! A more blessed death can never be yours, for you die in obeying
the divine Word ...' *Against the Robbing and Murdering Hordes of
Peasants* lost Luther considerable support among the poorer classes,
at least temporarily, but it firmly re-established his position among the
rulers who were inclined towards reform of the Church. Any damage
done by the activities of Hutten and Sickingen was more than
repaired. Not only was he clearly not hostile to the powers of the territorial rulers, as the Imperial Knights had been, but he was even
regarding them as God's ministers on earth.

c) Church Government

This stance was to be of major importance in the development of
Lutheranism. It meant that the reformed churches were going to be
supportive of the powers of the princes and were not going to set
themselves up as rival authority systems. As a result it became
tempting for any ruler in Germany, whether or not he was personally
committed to Luther's teaching, to declare in favour of the
Reformation. By doing so he could expect to free himself from the
political and financial intervention of the papacy, while gaining effective control of the Church within his territories.

Luther, in fact, was not greatly interested in the arrangements
made to ensure the supervision of the Church once the hierarchical

structure of bishops and archbishops had been removed. He understood that the demands of good order necessitated the introduction of some system but he was prepared to accept whatever was agreeable to his leading supporters and the princes. The structure that emerged clearly established the ruler as the 'head' of the Church within his territories in terms of both protection and regulation. This was not particularly to Luther's liking because he retained a preference for keeping temporal and spiritual authority in different hands, but it was not an issue that he considered to be in any sense vital.

An over-riding priority in his and others' minds was the maintenance of public order. There were few people able to make Luther's distinction between matters of fundamental belief, where uniformity was necessary, and less important issues, where it was not. To an overwhelming majority of the population uniformity in all aspects of religion was necessary. If each congregation were allowed to make its own decisions even on less important issues, it would certainly lead to strife and would probably result in civil war. It would therefore be necessary for the religious practices within any one state to be uniform, and for the Church to be regarded as containing the whole population, so that there would exist none of the differences that were likely to lead to communal violence. The only structure available to enforce this was the civil power. So, in electoral Saxony, the ruler was responsible for appointing a body of Visitors whose task it was to investigate the arrangements and practices of each parish. It was then for the Elector to ensure that the Visitors' decisions were implemented. Similar arrangements were made in other states as they adopted Lutheranism.

d) The Family

Luther's heavy emphasis on the citizen's duty to be obedient to his ruler was paralleled in his teachings on social relationships, where the family was seen to be of paramount importance. Just as the prince was the head of the state, so the father was the head of the family. It was his responsibility to impose discipline on his whole household, including wife, children and servants, and it was their duty to be obedient to him in all things. This did not preclude love and affection, as Luther's many letters to his wife show, but these operated within a clearly hierarchical relationship. Lutheranism has correctly been identified as fostering social conservatism. Its male chauvinism was, of course, an accurate reflection of the age.

Luther was one of the great theologians of his century. His fine mind and diligent application to study meant that he made few avoidable mistakes. But his touch was less sure on more practical matters where he sometimes displayed considerable naivety, and even folly. Such a case was the part he played in the bigamy of Philip, Landgrave of Hesse. After the death of Frederick the Wise in 1525, Philip of Hesse became the leading defender of the Protestant cause. He was a man of vacillating moods, at one moment a lusty sinner, the next a depressed penitent. He could find no sexual satisfaction with the wife to whom he had been married for dynastic reasons as a youth. But he was periodically overwhelmed by remorse over the string of mistresses he resorted to in her place. He concluded that his sexual and spiritual needs would be met if he were able to marry a woman whom he found physically attractive. Luther, and other leading Protestants who were consulted in 1540, advised him that, although divorce was out of the question, it would be acceptable for him to take a second wife if all involved were in agreement. The advice seems to have been based on Old Testament precedent. Philip acted on the advice. When news of the bigamous marriage leaked out, the part played by Luther was revealed. In an attempt to extricate himself from an impossible situation he knowingly lied. This in turn became common knowledge. His reputation was permanently damaged, and the political position of the Protestant cause was seriously weakened (see page 96).

This blunder was typical of Luther's actions in the years leading up to his death in 1546. He had become a petulant (and some would say, nasty) old man. But this should not be allowed to detract from his earlier enormous achievements. It should merely act as a reminder that long lives are rarely of one piece. Perhaps it is unreasonable to expect them to be so. Luther was a man with faults and failings but through the quality of his mind, the force of his personality, and the intensity of his religious convictions he was instrumental in changing the course of modern European history.

Working on Chapter 3

The notes you make on this chapter will be your record about Luther's teachings on religious beliefs and practices, and political and social issues. There is a lot of ground for you to cover so you are likely to write more on this chapter than on any other part of the book. Besides explaining what Luther's teachings were, you will need to make a record of why they were as they were, how important each issue was to Luther, and what the importance/significance of each issue was. You will also need to reach conclusions about the way in which Luther acted, especially about how far he was justified in acting as he did.

The simplest way to make notes which focus on Luther's teachings exclusively would be to work through the chapter dealing with each teaching as it arises. In each case you should start by identifying what the teaching was, and then should go on to comment on the other aspects listed in the last paragraph. This approach would undoubtedly involve you in more thinking for yourself than if you merely made notes on the chapter paragraph by paragraph, but the additional effort would be well worthwhile in ensuring that you thought about each issue rather than just paraphrasing what you had read.

Summary Diagram
Luther's Teachings

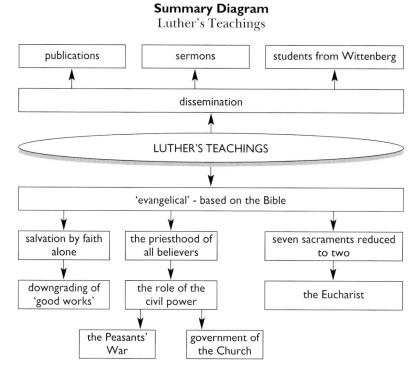

A less complicated way of making your notes, but one which would still require you to think for yourself, would be to work through the chapter writing answers to the questions in the issues boxes. In terms of ensuring maximum understanding of what you read, there is a strong argument in favour of adopting this approach for your note making throughout the book. However, if you adopt this strategy you must be prepared to reorganise the notes you make when you reach the revision stage so that they bring together all the factual details on each topic.

Answering structured and essay questions on Chapter 3

You have now completed the parts of this book which concentrate on Luther's personal contribution to the Reformation in Germany, although some further evidence can be found in Chapter 6. Now would therefore be a good time to prepare yourself for answering questions that focus specifically on 'the great reformer'.

It is very unlikely that you will ever be asked to write a narrative account of the whole of Luther's life, but you would be well advised to commit to memory the chronological 'shape' of his life so that you can select the relevant information for any particular question.

Structured questions on Luther's life are likely to require you to write about a mixture of what Luther did, why he did it, and what were the effects of his actions. Sometimes you will be asked to give your opinion on a controversial issue where there is no 'right' answer. In such cases it is vital that you supply evidence to back up your point of view. Look at the following question and identify for each part whether you are expected to deal with causes, course or consequences.

Luther and the German Reformation

a) What were the main stages by which Luther became a rebel against the Catholic Church?

b) Why did Luther come to the conclusion that he must leave the Church rather than work for changes from within it?

c) What were the main unintended effects that Luther's stand against the Church had? How far was Luther to blame for these effects?

Essay questions on Luther are often of the 'challenging statement' type, in which you are given a particular point of view to discuss. When examiners set this type of question they are not expecting you to agree with the opinion expressed unless you genuinely agree with it. What they are hoping for is that you will write about all of the important interpretations on the issue, indicating both what is the main evidence supporting each one and which interpretation you find the most convincing, and why. Make a plan, following this approach, for each of the three questions below.

1. 'Luther's main contribution to the Reformation in Germany was to encourage lay rulers to break from Rome.' Do you agree?

2. Discuss the opinion that 'Luther would not have left the Catholic Church if the Pope had not been so inflexible'.

3. Is it true that 'the single most important part of Luther's teaching was his belief in salvation by faith alone'?

A popular line of questioning about Luther concentrates on whether he was essentially a revolutionary or a conservative. The information from this chapter is most useful in answering such questions. Typical examples are:

4. 'The most conservative of revolutionaries'. Is this an accurate assessment of Martin Luther?

5. How true is it that 'Martin Luther was a conservative who could never foresee the consequences of his words and actions'?

6. In what sense would it be fair to describe Luther as a revolutionary?

Make two lists, one under the heading 'revolutionary' and one headed 'conservative'. You will find it helpful to use the sub-headings 'religious', 'political', 'social' and 'economic' in each list. What would be a useful way in which to further sub-divide 'religious'? When you decide which factors to put in which category, remember to consider both what is accurate and what some contemporaries mistakenly thought. Will you need to make a distinction between his early career (say, before 1525) and his later career?

Use the lists you have compiled to plan an answer to question **4**. Is it better to start with the ways in which he was a conservative, or the ways in which he was revolutionary? Why?

Source-based questions on Chapter 3

1. The Priesthood of all Believers
Read the extracts from *On the Babylonish Captivity of the Church* and *The Address to the German Nobility* on pages 42 and 43. Answer the following questions:

a) What argument, in the first extract, does Luther use to justify his rejection of the sacrament of orders? *(2 marks)*

b) What restriction does he place on the practical implications of his belief in the priesthood of all believers? *(2 marks)*

c) Explain the papal claim, referred to in the second extract, that has to do with St Peter and 'the keys' (line 5). *(4 marks)*

d) Is there any difference in tone between the two extracts? Explain your answer. *(3 marks)*

e) For what reasons was 'the priesthood of all believers' thought to be such a revolutionary belief? *(4 marks)*

2. Good Works
Read the extract from *Of the Liberty of the Christian Man* on page 44, and answer the following questions:

a) What does Luther mean by 'justification' (line 14)? *(2 marks)*

b) In what ways did Luther's teachings on 'good works' differ from those of the Church? *(4 marks)*

c) Why did some contemporaries believe that Luther's teachings on 'good works' endangered the maintenance of law and order? *(4 marks)*

3. The Peasants' War, 1525
Read the extracts from *Against the Robbing and Murdering Hordes of Peasants* on pages 55 and 56. Answer the following questions:

a) What are the implications of Luther's statement, in the first extract, that 'they have forfeited body and soul' (line 6)? *(2 marks)*

b) What is meant, in the second extract, by the phrase 'even though he does not tolerate the Gospel' (line 1)? *(2 marks)*

c) In the first extract Luther criticises the peasants on three counts. Which of these counts does Luther feel most strongly about? Explain your answer in detail. *(5 marks)*

d) What do the extracts show of Luther's views on i) the duties of rulers, and ii) the duties of subjects? With whom were these views likely to be popular? *(3 marks)*

e) What generalisations about the tone of Luther's writings do these extracts substantiate? *(3 marks)*

4 Zwingli

POINTS TO CONSIDER

This chapter concentrates on the ideas and actions of Ulrich Zwingli, an almost exact contemporary of Luther. As you read the chapter for the first time, attempt to identify the central idea behind Zwingli's beliefs and to find answers the question 'Why was it Luther rather than Zwingli who became the central figure in the early Reformation?'.

KEY DATES

1484 Zwingli born
1506 Zwingli became a parish priest at the young age of 22
1518 Zwingli moved to Zurich
1523 Zurich disputations
1529 The Marburg Colloquy
1531 Second War of Kappel, Zwingli killed in battle

1 Background

KEY ISSUES What did Zwingli believe and why? In what ways was Zurich potentially fertile ground for the spread of Zwingli's ideas?

We must make a conscious effort to avoid falling into the trap of believing that the early Reformation *was* Luther. Of course, Luther was the giant whose influence on events was enormous, but others were also of real significance, despite the fact that most historians correctly categorise them as 'minor characters'. Many of the 'minor characters' were essentially followers of Luther who acted as the focus of reform in their own localities. But some regarded themselves as being independent of the great reformer's influence. They tended to resent his assumed superiority.

The 'minor character' who exerted the greatest degree of independent influence was Ulrich (or Huldreich, or Huldrych - he used a variety of spellings of his name) Zwingli (1484-1531). Zwingli was born and bred, and lived almost all his life, in Switzerland, a loose confederation of 13 states (known as cantons) which, although almost totally German in ethnic background, was sufficiently remote and independent to be regarded as not being a part of Germany proper. There was a long-standing antipathy between Germans and Swiss. Germans looked down on the Swiss as being ignorant, poverty-stricken and uncivilised mountain dwellers. This view was not completely inaccurate, but it was greatly resented by the Swiss. There was therefore a natural tendency on the part of each to reject the opinions of the other. So it is not surprising that an independent Reformation took place in Switzerland.

Zwingli, like Luther, came from peasant stock. Also like Luther, he was picked out when young as a boy of outstanding intellectual ability. He was given a traditional education at school and university in preparation for a career in the Church. Thanks to the influence of other members of his family who had 'made good', he became a parish priest in the small town of Glarus at the early age of 22 in 1506. For ten years he continued in this role, combining the routine work of priest with intensive study, which was his real love. By 1516 his expertise in Latin, Greek and Hebrew was such that he was regarded as one of the foremost scholars in Switzerland. His particular interest was the Bible. When Erasmus published his edition of the New Testament in the original Greek in 1516, it was a revelation to Zwingli. As he studied it he became convinced that many of the teachings of the Church were either positively incorrect or clearly lacking in biblical justification.

Such conclusions were disturbing to Zwingli who had always assumed that the orthodox beliefs of his time contained divine truth. But slowly he had to admit to himself that the Church was seriously in error. This was a matter of the greatest importance, because, according to his understanding, the ordinary people, who relied on the Church for guidance, were being misled and were heading for eternal damnation. Unless they were taught correctly how to secure their salvation, they would go straight to hell when they died. According to Zwingli's beliefs the remedy was simple. He was certain that the Bible contained a complete statement of God's intentions for humanity. All that was necessary, therefore, was for the people to have explained to them what the Bible actually said. They could hardly avoid believing what was so obviously the word of God, and, in the process, they would be saved and God's will would be done. Thus Zwingli became a complete evangelical, believing that every religious issue was to be resolved by deciding on the correct interpretation of the Bible. What was not supported by the Bible was invalid.

In 1518 Zwingli moved to Zurich, the most powerful of the Swiss cantons. Zurich was essentially a city-state which had acquired large areas of the surrounding countryside by conquest. It was ruled by a council selected by generally democratic means. The Council regarded itself as having control over all aspects of life, including religion. Zwingli's influence in Zurich was therefore potentially immense if he could convince people of the correctness of his views. This he was in a good position to do as the post he had moved to was that of preacher. As preacher his sole duty was to teach the people. Traditionally preachers had expounded the teachings of the Church, but Zwingli concentrated entirely on explaining the Bible. He was not afraid to point out where the teachings of the Church appeared to be at fault.

Like the prosperous inhabitants of most German cities, the citizens of Zurich were generally very serious-minded. They were especially so over religious matters. In addition, they had sufficient independence of mind to think they were as likely to be right as were professional theologians. They respected the Pope as the head of the Church, but were not particularly in awe of him. In fact, when Zwingli arrived in the city, they were somewhat annoyed with the Pope as he was being very slow in paying for the mercenary troops which he had recently hired from Zurich. So, when Zwingli began to challenge the orthodox teachings of the Church, he was not automatically branded a subversive and banned from teaching. If anything, the reverse was true. He rapidly built up a large following among all classes of the population, including the rich and the powerful. He became a councillor, and within a short time a majority of the Council was in sympathy with his views.

2 The Reformation in Zurich

> **KEY ISSUES** What form did the Reformation in Zurich take? Why did it happen as it did?

From the outset Zwingli was at pains to insist to his audiences that no violence should be done to those who did not accept his interpretations of the Bible. Persuasion must be relied on at all times, because the uninformed could not be blamed for their state of ignorance. Therefore changes in religious practice were only brought about in Zurich slowly, as the majority became convinced of their necessity. But by 1523 it was clear that this gradualist approach was satisfying no one in the city. Those who favoured reform were becoming restless at the continuation of what they regarded as heretical practices, while orthodox Catholics could see no end to the challenge to their traditional beliefs.

So the Council decided to attempt to resolve the situation one way or the other. The decision was not to be made on the basis of what was politically advantageous, but according to what was shown to be the truth. They instructed that the issues should be debated before them so that they could decide which point of view was correct. But the outcome of the resulting Zurich Disputations of January and October 1523 was never in doubt. The representatives of the Catholic Church refused the invitation of the Council, stating that laymen had no authority to decide on religious matters. This left the way clear for Zwingli who was able to set out his beliefs (subsequently published as the *Sixty-seven Propositions*) almost unopposed. What had started out in 1518 as an attempt to bring about the reform of the Church had now reached the point where a break with Rome was unavoidable. This break came officially in 1525 when the mass was replaced by the

Zurich Council with a service that was unacceptable to the Pope. The rupture had only been delayed so long, of course, because the papacy had chosen to overlook earlier breaches of Church discipline, not wishing to alienate one of its few reliable political allies and sources of military support. There was also the need to concentrate attention on Luther.

Within the territories controlled by Zurich the changes of the Reformation took place with general support and without any social or political upheaval. The two principles which lay behind every change were that the Bible was the only source of religious authority, and that its interpretation was for every believer to take part in and for the legally constituted government to decide on. So, with a maximum of agreement and a minimum of disruption, priests were encouraged to marry; the rules on fasting were abandoned; the veneration of the Virgin Mary and the saints ceased; altars, images and paintings were removed from churches; monasteries were closed and their incomes were diverted to charitable causes; the mass was outlawed; and the Council became the final arbiter in all matters religious.

3 Attempts to Spread the Zurich Reformation

> **KEY ISSUE** Why did the attempts to spread the Zurich Reformation meet with so little success?

Unfortunately for the prospect of peace in Switzerland, most of the other cantons in the Confederation decided to resist the spread of the new teaching. This stance made Zwingli's original strategy untenable. He had thought that it would only be necessary for people to hear the Bible properly taught. He believed that they would then understand the errors of their previous practices and would join the reformed faith. But if evangelical preachers were not to be allowed access to the people of the other Swiss cantons they would not be able to bring the news that salvation was assured to every believer. This was unacceptable to Zwingli and the leading political figures in Zurich, especially once Berne, the other leading Swiss canton, decided to join the ranks of the reformers in 1528. Now only about one third of the Swiss population lived in cantons which had remained Catholic. Zwingli became convinced that, in order to save the souls of the misguided, evangelical preachers must be allowed to do their work in all parts of the Confederation, and that, if necessary, military force should be used to ensure it.

It soon became clear that the Catholic cantons would not accept their military inferiority and give way with good grace. Instead, they successfully set about finding foreign allies to support them. Despite Zwingli's persuasive powers, there was little enthusiasm in Zurich, and less in Berne, for starting a civil war. This was shown in 1529 when war was declared, known as the First War of Kappel. For a month the opposing armies faced each other, taking care to remain just inside their respective territories. The prospect of spilling one another's blood was enough to convince them that the best thing to do was to make peace and try to find a solution to the problem by diplomatic means. This proved impossible, neither side being prepared to give way, and in 1531 the Second War of Kappel took place. The forces of the Protestant cantons were casual in the extreme and were surprised by the speed with which the numerically inferior Catholic forces launched an attack. In what was no more than a skirmish, the Protestants were routed. Zwingli, who was one of many preachers in attendance, was killed. Now that the architect of the policy of confrontation was dead, Zurich was prepared to accept that each canton within the Confederation must be allowed to make its own religious arrangements, and the fighting stopped. Thus the expansion of the Zwinglian Reformation was halted. It lived on in northern Switzerland, and in neighbouring areas of southern Germany, before being largely overshadowed by the spread of Calvinism in the second half of the century.

4 Zwingli and Luther

> **KEY ISSUES** To what extent was Zwingli influenced by Luther's thinking? What efforts were made to resolve the dispute between Luther and Zwingli? How successful were these efforts?

Why, then, have historians been so interested in Zwingli? After all, the long-term effects of his 13 years in Zurich were fairly negligible. He did not found a movement that had widespread international repercussions, nor was his theological thinking particularly influential in the development of Protestantism. It is rather that his life and work provide historians with an illuminating case study which can be used to highlight aspects of the activities of Luther and Calvin. Zwingli was almost exactly contemporary with Luther, but because he came to public notice a little later than Luther there has always been the suspicion that his work was largely derivative. The extent to which Zwingli's thinking was independent of Luther's has been hotly debated. Historians have also been interested in understanding why it was Lutheranism rather than Zwinglianism that established itself as the dominant force in early Protestantism.

The parallels between Zwingli and Calvin are interesting, of course, because they both did their important work in the same small country. The debt owed by Calvin to Zwingli and the reasons why the younger man was so much more influential are discussed in another volume in this series (*Calvin and the Later Reformation*).

When Zwingli first came to prominence as an evangelical reformer and began to publish pamphlets to explain and support his views, he was labelled by his opponents as a Lutheran heretic. It was assumed that he had been converted by Luther's arguments and was one of the many disciples who were spreading the new beliefs throughout the German-speaking world. This assumption offended Zwingli greatly. He maintained that he had reached his conclusions independently. He recognised that there were many points of similarity but contended that these were purely coincidental. He claimed that when he first came to Zurich he:

> set forth how I would, if God willed, preach the Gospel written by Matthew without human additions or controversial comment. No one here knew anything about Luther except that something had been published by him about indulgences.

He later asked bitterly:

> Why did the Roman cardinal and representatives who were staying at that time in our city of Zurich begin to hate and want to ensnare me, not making me out to be a Lutheran until they knew that Luther was a heretic?

He argued that:

> 1 I began to preach before ever I heard Luther's name, and to that end I began to learn Greek ten years ago in order that I might know the teachings of Christ from the original sources. The Papists say, 'You must be Lutheran, you preach just as Luther writes'. I answer, 'I preach just as
> 5 Paul writes, why not call me a Pauline?' ... I will not bear Luther's name for I have read little of his teaching and have often intentionally refrained from reading his books. I will have no name but that of my captain, Christ, whose soldier I am, yet I value Luther as highly as any man alive.

Historians have not always been totally persuaded by Zwingli's protestations. However, there is now general agreement that it would be unfair to deny him his place as an independent thinker. It seems likely that even if Luther had not existed, Zwingli would have followed the reforming path he did. Yet the fact remains that on all important issues bar one the two men came to almost identical conclusions. While there is no evidence that Luther knew of Zwingli before his own thoughts were highly developed, Zwingli came into some contact with Luther's ideas and would have found it difficult not to be influenced by them. However, Zwingli claimed, not very convincingly, that his thinking owed nothing at all to Luther.

The Lutheran and the Zwinglian Churches always remained apart. This was despite the fact that considerable efforts were made to persuade the two leaders to reach an agreement. The leading peacemaker was Philip of Hesse in whose territory the geographical spheres of influence of Lutheranism and Zwinglianism met. He was eager to see the Protestants display a fully united front to Charles V and the

Catholic princes so that they would be deterred from attempting to destroy the reformed Churches with military might. Philip knew that the Protestants would stand little chance if they allowed themselves to be picked off one by one. But Philip's sense of political realism was not shared by Luther and Zwingli, each of whom was convinced that only his interpretation of the Bible was in accordance with God's wishes. Each was prepared to change his opinion if he could be convinced that he was wrong, but would not contemplate doing so for reasons of political expediency. They both thought that even if a failure to agree increased the chances of meeting a violent and early death in this life, it was preferable to risking eternal damnation.

In the mid-1520s both sides set out their points of view in publications which were distributed throughout the German-speaking world. Luther, as usual, laced his theological arguments with large helpings of virulent abuse aimed directly at Zwingli. In response Zwingli was markedly more restrained, and concentrated on the points at issue. The dispute revolved around the meaning of one phrase in the Bible, where Jesus is reported as saying when he broke the bread at the Last Supper, 'Eat, this is my body'. Luther's disagreement with the Catholic Church over the Eucharist has already been discussed (see pages 49-52). Luther's position was that the orthodox Catholic belief in transubstantiation - that the bread used in the mass actually became the flesh of Jesus during the service - was wrong. But he was adamant that Jesus' words were meant literally. His quarrel with the Catholics was that they were being too simplistic and were misunderstanding the way in which Christ's body was present in the bread. Zwingli went much further. He rejected the argument that Jesus had meant the words literally, and instead argued that the words had been used figuratively - that by 'is', Jesus had meant 'represents'. He poured scorn on the absurd lengths Luther had gone to in his efforts to show that his interpretation was defensible. In fact, the lengths are such that no one without a good grounding in theology can follow them.

The longer the dispute lasted, the more entrenched the two sides became. And the more Zwingli seemed to be having the better of the argument, the more determined Luther became to prove that he was right. In a final attempt to gain agreement, Philip of Hesse persuaded the two protagonists, along with a handful of leading supporters, to meet each other. The meeting took place in October 1529 in Philip's castle at Marburg, and the hope was that once Luther and Zwingli were face to face they would be able to argue through the issue that separated them and reach a common understanding. But Philip was to be disappointed. Neither reformer was able to convince the other. Nor were they prepared to accept that the other could be recognised as a 'good Christian'. The meeting, known as the Marburg Colloquy, was largely a failure.

In his letter to his wife announcing the outcome of the meeting, Luther indicates where the major difficulty lay:

Luther (on the right) disputes with Zwingli at the Marburg Colloquy.

> I ... our friendly conference at Marburg is now at an end and we are in
> perfect union in all points except that our opponents insist that there is
> simply bread and wine in the Lord's Supper, and that Christ is only in it
> in a spiritual sense. Today the Landgrave (Philip of Hesse) did his best
> 5 to make us united, hoping that even though we disagreed yet we should
> hold each other as brothers and members of Christ. He worked hard
> for it, but we would not call them brothers or members of Christ,
> although we wish them well and desire to remain at peace.

In a more detailed account of the meeting, given by Zwingli in a letter
he wrote to one of his supporters, a somewhat different impression is
given:

> I ... [We] entered the arena in the presence of the Landgrave and a few
> others - 24 at most; we fought it out in this and in three further sessions,
> thus making four in all in which, with witnesses, we fought our winning
> battle. Three times we threw at Luther the fact that he had at other times
> 5 given a different exposition from the one he was now insisting on of those
> ridiculous ideas of his ... but the dear man had nothing to say in reply -
> except, 'You know, Zwingli, that all the ancient writers have again and
> again changed their interpretations of passages of scripture as time went
> on and their judgement matured.' ... He conceded that the body of
> 10 Christ is finite. He conceded that the Eucharist may be called a 'sign' of
> the body of Christ. These are examples of his countless inconsistencies,
> absurdities and follies; but we refuted him so successfully that the
> Landgrave himself has now come down on our side, though he does not
> say so in the presence of some of the princes ... [He] has given permis-
> 15 sion for our books to be read with impunity, and in future will not allow
> bishops who share our views to be ejected from their place. ... The truth
> prevailed so manifestly that if ever a man was beaten in this world, it was
> Luther - for all his impudence and obstinacy - and everyone witnessed it,
> too, although of course the judge was discreet and impartial. Even so,
> 20 Luther kept on exclaiming that he hadn't been beaten etc.

Yet there had been positive outcomes from the Colloquy. Positive
agreement had been reached on all aspects of belief apart from the
nature of the presence of Jesus during the Lord's Supper, and
although Luther had refused to accept the Zwinglians as proper
Christians, he had undertaken not to attack them in print. So, at least
Philip had the comfort of knowing that his fellow Protestants would
not be at each other's throats.

5 Assessment

> **KEY ISSUE** Why is Luther considered to be of much more historical
> importance than Zwingli?

Thus it was clear by 1529 that Luther and Zwingli were in complete agreement on almost all issues. Their beliefs and attitudes were so similar, yet the place each occupies in history is so different. Luther is regarded as one of the most significant characters of the sixteenth century, while Zwingli is hardly remembered outside his own country. Why was there this great difference?

It is tempting to offer an explanation partly in terms of Zwingli's early death, which occurred just as he was reaching the peak of his influence. The primacy of his position in the religious affairs of Protestant Switzerland was established, and the Marburg Colloquy had further enhanced his reputation in southern Germany. It could be argued that had it been Luther who had died and Zwingli who had survived for a further 15 years or so, their roles might have been reversed. But such an argument would lack credibility. The two men shared common beliefs and pursued similar policies, but Luther towered above Zwingli in many respects.

Most obvious was the effect that Luther had on the people who met him. Because he was so clearly a man of charisma whom others could recognise as a 'superior being' without losing face, men of distinction in their own right were prepared to act as his supporters and, even, as his disciples. This allowed Luther's ideas to be spread widely through the good offices of local leaders who were personally committed to his stance. It also meant that many local leaders were prepared to abide by his judgement in matters of disputed theology, thus ensuring that the unified nature of the evangelical movement was largely maintained. Zwingli was never in a position to wield such personal authority. Although he was recognised as a man of great learning, few regarded him as being more than 'the first among equals'. He was never able to build up a band of devoted followers in the way that Luther did.

It was not only Luther's influence with local leaders, both lay and ecclesiastical, that marked him out from Zwingli. He was also able to establish a dominant position in the minds of ordinary people throughout much of Germany. This he did with the products of the printing press. Whereas Zwingli and his followers produced a trickle of publications, Luther, personally, produced a flood (see page 41). But the difference was not only one of quantity. It was also a matter of quality - fitness to purpose. Zwingli's writings were calm and clearly reasoned, while many of Luther's were couched in the rough and ready terms that appealed to the tastes and prejudices of the multitude. Luther's tracts were eagerly sought, widely bought and rapidly passed from hand to hand. Zwingli's were not.

Yet the natural advantages enjoyed by Luther should not be ignored, even though they do not explain why he is considered to be much more important historically than Zwingli. It is clear that even without these advantages Luther would have been the dominant figure of the Reformation in the German-speaking world. With them, his position was even more outstanding. Perhaps his greatest advantage was that he achieved fame (or notoriety, depending on your point of view), several years before Zwingli, who was therefore always following in his wake. Because their messages were so similar it was virtually impossible for Zwingli to create a distinct impact in areas where Luther's work was already known. So he found much of his 'natural market' already taken.

Luther was also fortunate in the geographical position of Saxony, his adopted state. From his base in Wittenberg his message could radiate to the thickly populated areas of Germany to the north, east, west and south-west. Proximity and relative ease of travel were important matters at a time when a journey of a few kilometres could be a major undertaking, and when news spread by word of mouth and ideas were shared in printed material that was often distributed by men on foot. Zwingli, of course, shared none of this advantage. He lived in a remote and mountainous region on the very edge of the German-speaking world. For his message to gain more than relatively local circulation was bound to take time, time in which Lutheranism had established itself as the Protestant orthodoxy of northern and eastern Germany, and rival leaders had grown up in southern Germany. So Zwinglianism had little scope for expansion outside Switzerland.

Nor did it have the trained personnel for such an expansion. Luther's work was centred on the university in Wittenberg. Hundreds of young men were attracted to it from all parts of Germany and beyond. Many of them returned to their native areas after several years of study during which they had become convinced Lutherans, and acted very much as unpaid missionaries. It is possible to trace the spread of Luther's ideas partly in terms of returning students from the University of Wittenberg. There was no university in Zurich, and Zwingli was killed before he could establish an effective mechanism for training recruits to his faith. He therefore had no pool of potential missionaries.

Zwingli was essentially one of the interesting 'might have beens' of sixteenth-century history. He shared with Luther what many have seen as a typically Germanic insistence that change must come in carefully planned stages and without public disturbance. He emphasised the need for discipline. As a result he led Zurich in a fundamental redirection of religious belief and practice which was achieved virtually without bloodshed or major discord. Had Luther not been a 'national' figure already, the pattern Zwingli established in Zurich might have been copied in much of northern Europe.

Working on Chapter 4

You need to make notes from this chapter on two distinct topics:

1. the life and teachings of Ulrich Zwingli, and
2. what can be learnt about Luther from his dealings with Zwingli.

Your notes on the life of Zwingli should be brief. An effective way of ensuring brevity is to make the notes in the form of a chronological table, allowing no more than two lines for any entry.

Making notes on the second topic is less straightforward as you will need to do a lot of thinking before you write. Whereas the chapter is written from Zwingli's point of view, your notes should look at the relationship the other way round, from Luther's side. Your aim is to record what his dealings with Zwingli illustrate about Luther. This can best be done by considering two different aspects separately: what Luther's dealings with Zwingli show about his teachings, and what they suggest about his personality and character.

Answering structured and essay questions on Chapter 4

You are most likely to be asked about Zwingli in a structured question. Although you should be prepared to give a brief and straightforward account of his life, you should also be ready to write about him analytically. Typical questions are those posed in the issues boxes within the chapter. It would be worthwhile spending some time thinking through how you would answer these.

You will rarely be given an opportunity to answer an essay question just on Zwingli, as it is generally thought unrealistic to expect you to know enough about him to be able to write at such length. When such questions arise they normally make up for their narrowness by being straightforward. So you could be asked to, '*Assess Zwingli's contribution to the Reformation*'. Look back to Chapter 3 for guidance on how to approach questions like this.

More probably you will be asked to compare Zwingli with someone else. The obvious candidates for comparison are, of course, Luther and Calvin. When you come to study Calvin, you will need to be aware of this possibility. Questions seeking comparisons tend to be wide-ranging, for instance, '*Compare Luther and Zwingli as religious reformers*'. The danger here is that you will have so much information available that you will be tempted to produce a long and unfocused narrative or description. To avoid this, you must carry out a careful analysis of the concept of a 'religious reformer' before you put pen to paper. You must compare the two men aspect by aspect. Obvious aspects to choose are, their teachings about beliefs, their teachings about practices, their methods of bringing about reform, and their success/influence. You will probably find it most straightforward to include similarities and differences on the same aspect within the same paragraph. A more ambitious approach would be to deal with similarities in one half of the essay, and differences in the other. It would be sensible to try this approach outside the examination room to see whether you can handle it.

Summary Diagram
Zwingli

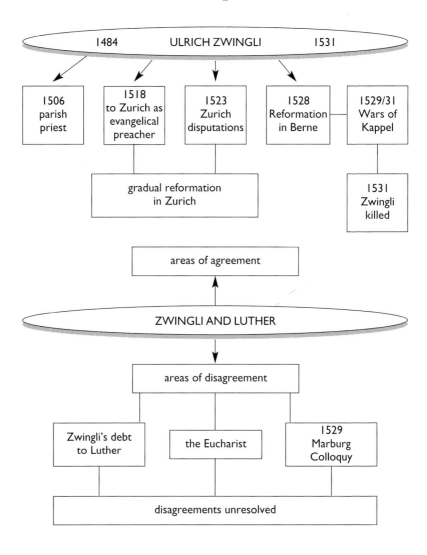

Source-based questions on Chapter 4

1. Zwingli's debt to Luther
Read the extracts from statements made by Zwingli on page 67. Answer the following questions:

a) What 'evidence' does Zwingli use to support his claim that his ideas owed nothing to Luther? *(3 marks)*

b) What were likely to have been Zwingli's motives in refusing to 'bear Luther's name', (line 5)? *(3 marks)*

c) What is the tone of these extracts? Explain your answer. *(4 marks)*

2. The Marburg Colloquy, 1529
Read Luther and Zwingli's accounts of the Marburg Colloquy on page 70 and study the illustration on page 69. Answer the following questions:

a) Over which issue did Luther and Zwingli fail to agree at Marburg? Explain their differing views on the issue. *(6 marks)*

b) Why did Philip of Hesse act in the way that is described? *(2 marks)*

c) Based on evidence contained in the extracts, which side had the best of the argument? Explain your answer. *(6 marks)*

d) What are the strengths and weaknesses of the extracts and the illustration as evidence of what actually happened at the Marburg Colloquy? *(6 marks)*

5 The Anabaptists

POINTS TO CONSIDER

This chapter is about the people who left the Catholic Church during the early Reformation without becoming part of either the Lutheran or the Zwinglian Churches. They are all described as being Anabaptists. However, this sharing of the same name should not be taken as indicating any organisational links between the various Anabaptist groups. As you read the chapter for the first time, try to identify what beliefs and practices most Anabaptists had in common. Also find answers to the question 'Why and with what justification were Anabaptists frequently feared by those in authority?'.

1 Background

KEY ISSUE Why have the Anabaptists largely been ignored by British and European historians?

Luther and Zwingli were the moderates of the Reformation. Many of their earliest supporters quickly became impatient with their caution. There was a demand for a much more radical break with old beliefs and practices. It was argued that the initial thinking had not been taken to its logical conclusion, and that it should be. Such views were increasingly expressed in Saxony and elsewhere from 1522 onwards. At first there was little coherence to the voices of discontent which were mainly expressions of individual opinion, but it soon became clear that there was a large number of people who shared a common view. They were not prepared to be bullied into silence. They believed that they were right and that they had been chosen by God as prophets to spread the truth. This they proceeded to do.

These radical religious reformers have been given the collective name of Anabaptists. The word was first used to describe Zwingli's radical opponents in Zurich in the mid-1520s but was soon made to apply to all those who advocated rapid and radical changes in religion. It drew attention to the fact that most of them practised adult baptism - Anabaptist means 'somebody who believes in baptism again' - as opposed to the infant baptism of the Catholics, the Lutherans and the Zwinglians.

Historians have traditionally taken little interest in the Anabaptists. They have been viewed as something of a lunatic fringe to the Reformation, occasionally intruding on the main flow of events, but rarely of any great significance. This is understandable. The radicals played little part in shaping the outcome of the Reformation; they founded no institutions that became important in later years; and they left no readily accessible body of records on which researchers could work. However, in recent decades a number of American historians have become interested in the Anabaptists. Many of them are members of modern-day religious groups which are descended from the Anabaptists. This has resulted in some serious and sympathetic work being done on the part played by the radical religious reformers in sixteenth-century European history. But much more will have to be done before prevailing attitudes will be changed. In the meantime, the tendency to dismiss the Anabaptists by lumping them together as insignificant extremists will continue.

Although it has always been clear that it is dangerous to make sweeping generalisations about such a disparate group as the Anabaptists, it is acceptable to draw attention to the common tendencies among them, as long as it is realised that there were always many exceptions to the rule. So it must be remembered that few individuals or congregations conformed to all the features described as being typical of the Anabaptists. Yet such generalisations must be made if any understanding is to be gained of how the radicals differed from the 'main-line' Protestants.

2 Distinguishing Features

> **KEY ISSUE** What marked out the Anabaptists as different from other Christian groups?

Luther, Zwingli and their leading followers were evangelicals. They broke with Rome essentially because they were certain that what they thought of as God's Word, as revealed in the Bible, should always take precedence over the traditional teachings of the Church. Their approach was academic. They were scholars struggling to find the true meaning of a difficult text, and squabbling viciously over rival interpretations. Despite all their talk of faith, they were very intellectual, relying greatly on logic at the expense of the emotions. The Anabaptists, few of whom thought of themselves as scholars, did not regard the Bible as paramount. They believed that God communicated directly with the individual believer by way of the Holy Spirit. They accepted that this could occur while the Bible was being studied, but were equally prepared to recognise the validity of visions and inner voices. Most of them acknowledged these communications as the real Word of God, even when they were in direct conflict with the Bible message. Some of them even thought of the Bible as a work of the Devil, designed to ensnare the unwary in Satan's web. They were therefore very vulnerable to the lunatic ravings of skilful demagogues who claimed to be God's specially chosen messengers, and the worst excesses occurred when such men built up a large body of support.

The Anabaptists were not original in adopting a more spiritual approach to religion. For more than a century voices had been raised against the emphasis placed by the Church on the performance of religious rites rather than on the beliefs that people held. Luther had gone some way towards establishing a balance between the importance attached to what one believed and what one did, but the radicals went much further. A small minority of them taught that belief was all important and that behaviour did not matter. This was taken by some as a justification for attempting to satisfy all their appetites. Many Anabaptists also followed a long-established tradition of millenarianism - the belief that the end of the world and the second coming of Jesus, as predicted in the Bible, were near at hand. This belief led some to think that they had nothing to do but to wait patiently for the inevitable to happen and for the Kingdom of God to come into being. Others were persuaded that the Second Coming would only take place once all non-believers were dead. They therefore set about what they understood was God's work, with swords in hand and clear consciences. They aimed to wash away the sins of the world with the blood of the wicked.

This division of humanity into the saved and the damned was general among Anabaptists. The saved were those who agreed totally with the beliefs of the group of Anabaptists making the judgement: the damned were those who differed. Toleration was therefore no more common among radicals than it was among Catholics or other Protestants. In fact, it tended to be less in evidence. Whereas moderate Christian groups such as the Lutherans and Zwinglians accepted a definition of the Church that allowed the total population into membership, the Anabaptists believed that only those who were true believers, and who had witnessed their belief in adult baptism, should be allowed entry. They were also determined to protect the purity of their congregations by expelling those who showed themselves to be less than fervent in their beliefs. The Anabaptists therefore formed themselves into exclusive groups which presented, at best, an unwelcoming face to outsiders.

The exclusiveness was not restricted to the performance of religious practices. Most Anabaptists regarded the world as a wicked place, full of temptation, and they tended to turn their backs on it. They tried to mix only with fellow believers as these were likely to support them in their particular code of behaviour. This often meant removing themselves physically from the rest of the community and withdrawing into self-contained units. Even if they remained in contact with the mass of unbelievers, they marked themselves out as being very different. Sometimes this was done by adopting simplified forms of dress or purified forms of speech, but more often it was a matter of adopting a totally different life-style, revolving around hard work, few pleasures and frequent worship. Piety - later to be labelled puritanism - was their major distinguishing feature. The undeserved reputation they sometimes have for gluttony, drunkenness and sexual licence was acquired as the result of the actions of some atypical groups in the 1520s and 1530s.

Equally, it is misleading to describe them as violent. It is true that several hundred radical priests fought alongside the peasants during the war of 1524-25, and there certainly were cases of Anabaptist groups trying to rid the world of all sinners, but these were exceptional events, confined to the early years of the Reformation. For most Anabaptists non-violence was a deeply held principle. Not only did they generally not attack others, but most of them were not even willing to defend themselves from attack. They interpreted literally the commandment 'Thou shalt not kill', and regarded their sufferings at the hands of others as God's punishment of them for the sins they had committed.

This refusal to accept the killing of others in any circumstances was in effect a denial of the traditional view, strongly upheld by Luther, that the civil authorities had a God-given responsibility to ensure the maintenance of law and order and to punish wrong-doers. In fact, most Anabaptists refused to recognise any authority except that of God. They were therefore unwilling to do anything to support what they regarded as a usurpation of power by the civil authorities. They were not prepared to pay taxes, to serve in the army, to hold any public office, or to swear an oath of allegiance. They acted as if civil government did not exist.

3 Reactions to the Anabaptists

> **KEY ISSUE** Why were those in authority almost uniformly hostile to the Anabaptists?

It is not surprising that the Anabaptists were unpopular with the rich and the powerful. Their beliefs were seen as undermining the very basis of society, and it was rightly feared that they were encouraging the spread of civil disobedience and the breakdown of traditional methods of maintaining law and order. Their very existence threatened riot and discord because their assumption of spiritual superiority was guaranteed to inflame passions to such a point that popular hatred of them was almost certain to result in violence. Even Luther and Zwingli, with their desire to proceed by gentle persuasion, came reluctantly to accept that the Anabaptists were too disruptive a force to be allowed to remain alive, and agreed to advocate their execution if they refused to abandon their beliefs. So Anabaptists were persecuted wherever they were found. Many thousands of them were executed, mainly, but not exclusively, in Catholic states. Those living in Protestant communities were normally expelled rather than killed. But nowhere, except in remote and sparsely populated areas of Bohemia, were they allowed to remain openly for long. They did establish and maintain a few tightly disciplined and secretive communities in the Netherlands, but generally they were hounded from pillar to post. As a result it has not been easy for historians to piece together an accurate picture of what happened to them. At present there is insufficient evidence to support more than very generalised and tentative conclusions. But as more research is done it should become possible to chart the progress of many of the groups - of which there were probably more than a thousand, some of which existed for a few years, and some of which survived for generations - that are currently classified under the Anabaptist label.

At the same time it should be possible to correct the imbalance brought about by the existence of several well-documented and widely known examples of disreputable behaviour on the part of Anabaptists. These cases, which were extensively publicised, added greatly to the fear and hatred of the religious radicals that was present in almost all civil authorities at the time. They have also been largely responsible for the bad press received by the Anabaptists ever since.

Thomas Muntzer (1489-1525) was the most notorious of the early radical-revolutionaries. He was a parish priest who became one of Luther's early supporters in Saxony. But he quickly became disillusioned with his leader's caution and lack of interest in political and social issues. In 1521 he broke with Luther and started out on a brief career as a rabble-rouser, preaching that the second coming should be hastened by destroying the wicked, whom he largely equated with the rich. He argued that their possessions should be confiscated and redistributed among the poor. Frederick the Wise's famed reluctance to punish any preacher until a clear case against him was proved allowed Muntzer to argue his beliefs unhindered for three years. In the process he quite naturally spread alarm among the well-to-do. He also attracted a large amount of adverse publicity for the reforming cause, especially when he preached a typically extreme sermon before two of Frederick's closest relatives who had been sent to investigate the reliability of the hostile reports about him. Exile rapidly followed. But Muntzer was not yet finished. The coming of the Peasants' War in 1524 allowed him to practise what he had preached. He became one of the leading exponents of the mindless violence and destruction against which Luther published his much misunderstood diatribe *Against the Robbing and Murdering Hordes of Peasants* (see page 55). After leading his supporters to military defeat, he was captured, brutally tortured, and killed in 1525. His irrational hatred of the whole of the established order was in no sense typical of the religious radicals, but it has frequently been described as if it was.

Even more bizarre and damaging to the Anabaptists' reputation were the events that took place in the north-western German city of Munster during 1534 and 1535. A group of extremists of the Thomas Muntzer type managed to convert the city's leaders to their cause. They then offered a rare safe haven to social revolutionaries of all kinds, and especially to those who believed that blood must flow before Jesus would come again. Citizens who did not share their enthusiasm fled or were killed. The reaction of neighbouring princes, clerical and secular, Catholic and Protestant, was uniformly hostile. A combined army was raised and Munster was put under siege.

It was what happened during the year it took to starve the city into surrender that has been most reported. Jan Bockelson, a Dutch tailor, established a dictatorial hold over the population. He declared himself king, and established what he imagined to be an Old Testament regime of splendour, with every luxury that the city could provide. The surplus of women was solved by the introduction of compulsory polygamy. Law and order disappeared, unless at the whim of King Jan. The strong abused the weak. Full vent was given to all types of vice. All this was, of course, typical only of the small minority of Anabaptists who believed both that the end of the world was nigh, and that it did not matter what you did in the meantime because God had already decided whether or not you would be saved. The educated or rich person's fear that civilisation was only skin deep, and was constantly in danger of destruction, seemed to have been confirmed. When the city was at last taken, the besieging forces took great pleasure in hunting down and killing every survivor. It was almost a ritualistic cleansing after defilement. It was as if Anabaptism was a plague, all trace of which had to be eliminated before people could feel relatively safe again. For the rest of the century mention of Munster was sufficient to provoke in most people instant and unthinking hostility towards the religious radicals.

4 Conclusion

Yet Anabaptists continued to win converts and managed to maintain many of their congregations despite all the persecution. In some areas, especially in the northern parts of the Netherlands which became the United Provinces (Holland), considerable numbers of them lived in relative tranquillity, thanks to the willingness of sympathetic local magistrates to turn a blind eye to their existence. But this only lasted as long as they kept themselves to themselves and did not antagonise their neighbours. It was by becoming almost invisible, which was only possible in large urban areas, that most Anabaptist groups escaped destruction. Those that were not swallowed up by the spread of Calvinism during the second half of the century ensured the continuation of their particular beliefs only by exporting them to North America with some of the earliest settlers.

Many of the Anabaptist groups offered a theology that was as coherent and as spiritually satisfying as that presented by Catholicism or Lutheranism. Yet they were not able to mount a sustained challenge for dominance in a period when there was no middle position. There could only be winners or losers in the struggle of the religions. Religious toleration was widely regarded as undesirable and unworkable. Freedom of conscience was only to become a popular rallying cry in the late eighteenth century. The failure of Anabaptism to establish itself as the orthodoxy in any but small, local areas was partly the result of the fragmentary nature of the movement, which led to it having no overall coherence, and partly the result of its members' general refusal to become involved in the struggle for political power. It was also because of the political advantages that Lutheranism enjoyed.

Working on Chapter 5

It would be useful if your notes contained your own definition of the word 'Anabaptist'. This definition needs to be more than a single sentence. You should explain both the range of beliefs and practices covered by the word Anabaptist and why it is dangerous to make generalisations about the Anabaptists.

Anabaptists are often portrayed as being the lunatic fringe of the early Reformation. You need to decide whether or not you accept this judgment. This could be done by using the question 'Were the Anabaptists the lunatic fringe of the early Reformation?' as your heading and making your notes under the two sub-headings 'yes' and 'no'. Finish off your notes by writing a brief conclusion giving a direct answer to the question.

Studying the Anabaptists is a useful way of providing a perspective to your work on Luther. Divide a sheet of paper into two columns, one headed 'Anabaptists' and the other headed 'Luther'. In the 'Anabaptists' column enter the ten most important facts you know about the Anabaptists, starting each one on a new line. Ensure that you cover the three issues of beliefs, practices and organisation. In the second column enter for each fact Luther's policy on the same issue. Make your final entry a conclusion that can be drawn from the comparison.

Answering structured and essay questions on Chapter 5

As is the case with Zwingli, you are most likely to be asked about the Anabaptists in a structured question. You may be expected to provide a straightforward description of the Anabaptists' beliefs and practices, but it is more likely that you will be asked to write analytically. A good way of preparing to do this is to think through the questions posed in the issues boxes of this chapter. It would also be helpful to plan an answer to the following question:

a) What beliefs and practices did most sixteenth-century European Anabaptists share in common?
b) Why did these beliefs and practices frighten many rulers?
c) How far was fear of the Anabaptists justified?

Essay questions requiring knowledge about the Anabaptists are sometimes set. Occasionally questions deal exclusively with the Anabaptists, but more often they demand that you compare the

Summary Diagram
The Anabaptists

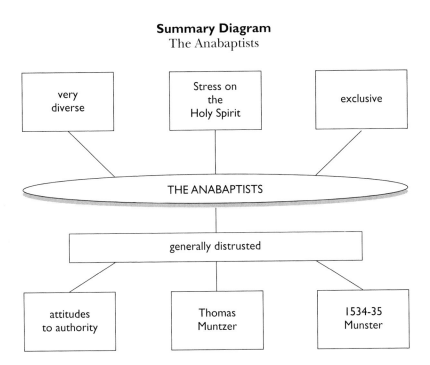

Anabaptists with the Lutherans. Look at the following two questions.

1. 'The Anabaptists failed to establish themselves permanently and widely in any European state because they were seen as a threat to the established social and political order'. Is this an adequate explanation of the Anabaptists' failure?

2. 'Luther and the Anabaptists differed on every important issue.' Discuss.

You will recognise both of these questions as being of the 'challenging statement' type. So your answers will be made up of two parts - 'Yes, the statement is true/accurate in these respects ...', and 'No, the statement is untrue/inaccurate in these respects ...'. In your conclusion you will state which part is, in your view, nearest to the truth.

As always, the skill required in planning an effective answer to this sort of question is the ability to identify the best way of structuring your material. For the first question this is to be done by deciding which are the 'issues' to be considered. Make a list of these. For the second question you will need to list the possible causes/explanations of the Anabaptists' failure. How would you decide the order in which to deal with these? Would you start with the strongest argument or would you leave this to last?

6

The Politics of Lutheranism

POINTS TO CONSIDER

This chapter considers reasons for the survival of Luther and Lutheranism after the Edict of Worms (1521). You need to weigh up the relative importance of impersonal factors, such as the political situation in Germany, and the actions of individuals, especially Frederick the Wise and Charles V. As you read the chapter for the first time, identify the 'impersonal factors' and decide which were temporary and which applied to the whole of the period 1521-55.

KEY DATES

1521 Luther went into hiding in the Wartburg
1525 Albrecht of Hohenzollern became a Lutheran
1526 Philip of Hesse became a Lutheran
1529 Diet of Speyer - origin of the word 'Protestant'
1530 Diet of Augsburg - Augsburg Confession drawn up
1531 League of Schmalkalden formed by Protestant rulers
1534 Ulrich restored to Dukedom of Württemberg
1547 Battle of Mühlberg - Protestants defeated by Charles V
1555 Peace of Augsburg

1 Why did Luther Survive?

KEY ISSUE Which was more important in ensuring Luther's survival, the actions of Frederick the Wise or the limitations on Charles V's powers?

In May 1521, when Martin Luther disappeared while returning from the Diet of Worms, he was theoretically a social outcast. He had been placed under the Imperial ban, meaning that all his rights to protection were forfeit. All citizens of the Empire were required to assist in his detention if they could. It would be no crime to kill him. This was an extremely serious situation. Frederick the Wise was not being over-cautious in insisting that Luther disappear totally from public view. He even made it clear that this might not be enough, and that it might be necessary to surrender him to the Emperor if the political pressure became too intense. It was unusual for any individual to survive for long once they had been placed under the Imperial ban. But Luther did. He lived in Saxony, free from arrest, for the next twenty-five years. Why was he able to do this?

Clearly he owed much, especially in the early years, to the support he received from his local ruler, Frederick, the Elector of Saxony. Not only did Frederick purposely fail to implement the terms of the Edict of Worms (see page 36), he actually provided Luther with a safe sanctuary in one of his castles, the Wartburg, while attempts were made to retrieve the political situation. Frederick's support was unwavering, even when it would have been expedient for him to fall into line with the wishes of Charles V and a large majority of the German princes. By his refusal to surrender Luther, Frederick risked upsetting the delicate balance of power that existed in Germany between the Emperor and the territorial rulers. There was a real danger that Charles would use the lack of co-operation on the part of the Elector as an excuse to invade Saxony, and even to depose him. Frederick had little to gain and much to lose from his support of Luther. It was not even as if he was a convinced follower of Luther's teachings. Right up to his death in 1525 he remained a notional Catholic. He was slow to abandon the sale of indulgences and to accept the spiritual worthlessness of the huge number of holy relics he had so assiduously collected. He was unprepared to take action until he was convinced of its correctness and that often took years. But he did keep an open mind in the meantime. While there was a good chance that Luther *might* be right he was unwilling to abandon him.

Had Luther been living in the territory of a minor prince his fate might have been different. There were few rulers who could expect to ignore an Imperial Edict without the direst of penalties being exacted. But Frederick was in a very strong position. As one of the seven Electors of the Empire he was a member of an elite group of territorial rulers whose influence was considerable. The Emperor required their agreement before he could take action of any significance, and he was careful not to upset them without very good reason. Frederick was also the ruler of a state that was relatively large and wealthy, and consequently well able to defend itself. So he was difficult to threaten convincingly. Yet this might have been insufficient had it not been for his personal standing. Epithets such as 'the Wise' were not easily acquired, and it seems to have been justified in Frederick's case. He was generally regarded as the outstanding ruler in Germany, and as a man whose judgement was to be respected. When, before the election of Charles V, there had been behind-the-scenes scheming to break the hold of the Habsburgs on the imperial title, it had been Frederick's name that had been put forward as the one likely to command general support. He was a powerful friend for Luther to have. The Emperor would be loath to take action against him.

Frederick was a skilful politician. He used all the advantages of his position to make it difficult for Charles to act decisively. He was particularly careful to ensure that he never left himself without room to manoeuvre. He always suggested a positive way forward rather than responding to Charles with a definite refusal. His main tactic was to argue that Luther's teachings should be given more careful consideration than they had so far received. He appealed to the widespread feelings of resentment at the Italian domination of the Catholic Church by suggesting that the issue should be decided in Germany at a Council of the German Church. This seemed a reasonable suggestion to most Germans, especially as it came from one of their most respected leaders who constantly maintained that his desire was to see the reform of abuses within the Church, not the establishment of an alternative organisation. In calling for a Church Council to be summoned in Germany, Frederick was resurrecting a demand that had frequently been heard in the past, and that had always been evaded by the papacy which claimed to be solely responsible for making decisions on matters of both belief and practice. He was purposely confusing the issue by linking Luther's cause with long-felt national resentments. And all the time he presented himself as a reasonable person seeking for a reasonable solution, which is essentially what he was.

Frederick's contribution to Luther's cause was great, especially in terms of ensuring that there was sufficient time and space in which it could gain support. But there were other contributory causes to Luther's survival. The very nature of the situation favoured him. In the politics of the Empire during the sixteenth century, inertia was the norm. The difficulty was to get anything done. Charles's task was, therefore, considerably more difficult than Luther's, for Charles had to gain agreement to action being taken, while Luther merely had to ensure that nothing happened. With poor communication systems, a civil service that was only embryonic, and a complex series of vested interests, the advantage clearly lay with Luther. The determined prevaricator or the skilful manipulator was always likely to triumph in dealings with higher authority.

To make matters worse for Charles, he was constantly faced with conflicting priorities. In some ways the fact that he ruled over such an extensive but fragmented personal empire, stretching from central Europe to the Americas, was a cause of weakness and not of strength. He was unable to give sufficient attention to even the emergency situations that arose with monotonous regularity, let alone to tackle the structural defects that made his territories in many ways ungovernable. He would have liked to remain in Germany to follow up the Edict of Worms by ensuring that his instructions were faithfully carried out, but he was forced to travel to Spain to deal with rebellions against him there. He did not return to Germany until 1529. In addition, for much of his reign, he was engaged in a struggle with France for predominance in European affairs. This led to long and costly wars, mainly fought in northern Italy, which demanded much of his attention.

Charles was also forced to divert his energies from time to time to stemming the flood of Ottoman expansion. Not only did he need to take action to prevent the Mediterranean becoming dominated by the Turks but, more seriously, he had to face the possibility that portions of the Holy Roman Empire itself would fall under the control of Muslims as the Ottoman Empire expanded through the Balkans to threaten his family's - the Habsburgs - homelands in Austria. This was significant in relation to the survival of Luther and Lutheranism in more than its value as a distraction to Charles. It also meant that he was forced to compromise with the Lutheran princes in order to win their support for the struggle with the Turks. When he should have been punishing them for their defection from Catholicism, he was actually agreeing to their continued heresy as the price to be paid for their military support. It was not that he was hypocritical when he stated that he saw it as his duty to defend the unity and purity of the Catholic Church. This was clearly an important motivating force for him throughout his reign. The problem was that Luther often seemed to be almost the least of his worries.

However, there were times when Charles devoted all his attention to the problem of the Lutherans. But he was still able to achieve little. He was constantly entangled in the perennial and contentious issue of the extent to which the Emperor had the right to interfere in the internal affairs of the territories which made up the Empire. The Emperor had been unable to establish anything like the same degree of authority in Germany as the Kings of France, England and Spain had acquired in their kingdoms. And the territorial rulers of Germany were determined to see that this situation did not change. They regarded themselves as being, to all intents and purposes, autonomous rulers of their states, with the right to order things much as they wished within their own borders. Therefore, when Charles attempted to act against those rulers who supported Luther, he found that the Catholic princes, who should have been his natural allies, were often lukewarm to his cause. They were both jealous of the ruler's right to do as he wished within his own territory, and fearful that a marked increase in the Emperor's power might result from a successful assault on the centres of Lutheranism. They suspected that any army used to restore religious orthodoxy would subsequently be used to impose Charles's will on all the states of the Empire.

This political division within the ranks of the Catholics ensured that there would be no speedy resolution of the problem of Luther. But, of course, it did not make certain the establishment of a permanent and separate Lutheran Church. That only happened because Luther, his supporters and his allies were able to capitalise on the long breathing space that Frederick the Wise's manoeuvrings and Charles V's difficulties allowed them.

2 The Establishment and Spread of Lutheranism in Germany

KEY ISSUES What was the process by which Lutheranism became accepted in a local area? Why was it that this process, once started, was rarely stopped?

When Luther disappeared from public view in May 1521, there was no such thing as Lutheranism. What existed throughout Germany was a large but uncounted body of supporters, most of whom were unknown to him personally. The priests and scholars among them had been won over by his theological publications which, for many, provided convincing answers to problems of belief that had long troubled them. To the lay people from all levels of society, from the prince to the peasant, who regarded him in some sense as a hero, his appeal was often that he challenged the abuses within the Church. He offered the prospect of relief from the financial demands of greedy clerics locally, and of the Pope nationally. But few, including Luther, had even thought of establishing a new Church. Their aim was the reformation of the one Church - the Catholic Church - that was known to them. This they expected to do from inside its ranks.

However, they did not intend to wait for agreement from Rome before proceeding. Wherever enough local support could be gained for a change in practices, be it the removal of paintings and images from churches, the abandonment of the rules of fasting, or some other matter, action was taken. This was sometimes done with the agreement of the local ruler, but more often it happened because he was powerless to prevent it. In hundreds of towns and villages in all parts of Germany an unofficial Reformation of this type was begun. It was unco-ordinated and very variable in outcome. In some places the changes were reversed once those in authority at a distance were able to make their power effective in the locality. But many rulers were at least benevolently neutral. In their territories little was done to inhibit the spread of reformed practices if that was what the people wanted. In some places these early changes were well documented. In most they were not. Fortunately for historians, there is plenty of evidence on the happenings in Wittenberg where, of course, Luther was personally very involved, although at a distance initially.

It seems that events there followed the general pattern that became common throughout the reforming towns and cities of Germany when efforts were made to translate Luther's theology into practice. A small group of reformers, often led by a priest who had read many of Luther's writings, would attempt to persuade the uncommitted majority that changes should be introduced. This was often done through public sermons. The force of their enthusiasm would frequently be sufficient to win enough support to allow them to proceed. Changes would be introduced and any objectors would be intimidated by threats of popular violence. The reformers would rarely agree among themselves on matters of detail, and would often refer their disputes to Luther for settlement. Even then there would often be some who refused to abide by the verdict, and who would choose to move on to another town rather than to remain and perform practices with which they could not agree. In this way reforming ideas would be brought to places that knew little of them, and the process would continue.

In Wittenberg this all happened in 1521-2 while Luther was in the Wartburg. Churches were cleansed of images; the mass was performed partly in German, with the congregation receiving the wine as well as the bread; the 25 priests who did nothing but perform masses for the dead were forced to cease their work; priests married; monks were persuaded to abandon their vows and to leave their monasteries; and riot was used to intimidate those who objected. Frederick attempted to slow things down by forbidding further change until general agreement had been gained. However, the reformers largely ignored him, and the town council took it upon itself to overrule the Elector and to invite Luther to return to Wittenberg. This he willingly did, although he understood that Frederick would do nothing to protect him were he to be arrested by anyone loyal to the Emperor. Luther's personal influence was such that he soon persuaded most of the town's leading citizens that change must come much more slowly, and only when its need was widely accepted. At this, some of the most active reformers left the town to seek a more sympathetic environment elsewhere. Among their number was Andreas Carlstadt, one of Luther's fellow professors at the university and one of his earliest supporters.

Similar events took place in hundreds of cities, towns and villages during the next three years. Most of the reformers looked to Luther for leadership, although in south-west Germany there was a marked tendency for them to go their own way. Luther readily responded to the many requests for advice, receiving numerous delegations, writing enormous numbers of letters, and publishing treatises on the most widely debated issues. He was especially quick to respond in print to those who disagreed with him on interpretations of the Bible, however trivial the differences appeared to be. Thus his influence on events sprang from his informal natural authority. He had established no formal links with the general body of evangelical reformers throughout Germany.

How, then, was this random and unorganised collection of reformed communities able to maintain itself in the face of the hostility of the Emperor? The answer lies partly in the extent and the depth of the popular support for Luther and the reformation. By the mid-1520s it would have been necessary to execute tens of thousands of Protestants before the primacy of Catholicism could have been restored. But, although this would have been difficult, it would not have been impossible, as had been shown in earlier centuries when widespread heresy had been exterminated by massacring whole populations. A not greatly dissimilar approach was adopted in Germany itself in 1525 at the end of the Peasants' War. So the deciding factor must have been the one that prevented a crusade being mounted against the Protestants.

This factor was the support gained from a large number of territorial rulers and ruling bodies. It was not merely that these acted as a delaying mechanism in Imperial deliberations, which was a vital factor in the years immediately following the Diet of Worms. It was also that they increasingly became totally committed to the Lutheran cause, in a way that Frederick the Wise never did. By 1525 many districts, especially those near to Saxony, were a complex mixture of Catholic, Lutheran and radical congregations. To further complicate matters, there were great variations even between congregations of the same general type. The situation was chaotic and, given the values of the time, unacceptable. It was an accepted truth in early sixteenth-century Europe that within any one state there could be only one set of religious arrangements if good public order was to be maintained. So it became necessary for rulers with a majority of reformed communities within their territories to consider the possibility of compelling all their subjects to become Lutherans.

The first prince to take this step was Albrecht of Hohenzollern, Grand Master of the Teutonic Knights. The Teutonic Knights belonged to one of the military orders that had been established by the Church in the middle ages to recapture territory from the pagans who were threatening Christendom from all sides. They had resisted Slav encroachment into eastern Germany and had gained control of part of modern-day Poland. In 1525 Albrecht became a Lutheran. He then, on Luther's advice, dissolved the Order unilaterally and declared himself to be the hereditary ruler of the Order's lands, with the title of Duke of Prussia. This somewhat untypical 'first' was followed by declarations for Lutheranism by princes closer to the Protestant heartland. The way was led in 1526 by Philip of Hesse, who was to regard himself as the political leader of the Protestant cause for the next 20 years. Frederick the Wise's successor, John, was also prepared to commit himself, and by 1527 Electoral Saxony was effectively Lutheran. Several other princes rapidly followed his example. Although their states were not always very large - as was the case with the Count of Mansfeld in whose territory Luther had been born - they constituted a significant political force within the Empire. But they were far outnumbered by the group of Imperial Cities which became Lutheran by the end of the decade. This group contained many of the major trading and wealthy financial centres of Germany. Their prestige was great and their power was considerable. They were generally well able to protect themselves, having city walls that were largely invulnerable to the military technology of the time. There were about 85 cities whose claim to Imperial City status, whereby they were subject to no authority but the Emperor's, was generally recognised. Over 50 of these declared in favour of the Reformation, although not all accepted the label of Lutheranism. With such a solid basis of effective political support, it was clear by the late 1520s that Protestantism could only be destroyed at the cost of a major civil war. This would be very different from the Peasants' War in which all those in authority had been united against brutal and rebellious subjects. This would be a matter of the

Emperor attempting to force his will on many of his leading subjects by military might. Charles could expect to receive little support in this.

The fact that so many princes and Imperial Cities were prepared to accept the Reformation publicly was remarkable. The only reasonable explanation appears to be that the people concerned believed strongly in the reformed faith, and were prepared to accept the consequences of their beliefs. This, of course, is not to deny that many of them wer also motivated by greed and self-interest.

The likelihood that self-interest was a major motivating force is strengthened when one considers what happened outside Germany. Lutheranism won converts in almost every Christian state of Europe, but only in Sweden and Denmark did it become the established Church, as it was to do in so many German states. In France, Spain, England, the Netherlands and Italy, the Lutheran converts were either killed, forced to flee or forced into hiding. The difference is only explicable in terms of the varying attitudes of the rulers. In Sweden a king, Gustavus Vasa, who was struggling to establish himself, was desperately in need of additional finance. By accepting the Lutheran Reformation in 1527 he was able to seize all of the Church's extensive lands. In Denmark a king, Christian III, whose right to the crown was seriously challenged, gained widespread support in the 1530s by adopting Lutheranism and ousting the existing rich, powerful and greatly hated churchmen. In contrast, the other rulers in western Europe had no need to espouse the new religion. They already had considerable power over the Church within their territories, and they had no need to ally with the middle ranks in society - from which much of Luther's support was drawn - against an overpowerful aristocracy, as was the case with Gustavus Vasa and Christian III. Even within Germany a similar pattern is discernible. In southern Germany where Charles V and his Habsburg relatives were very influential, Lutheranism was kept in check.

3 The Search for a Solution

> **KEY ISSUES** What efforts were made to reach agreement between Lutherans and Catholics in Germany? Why were these efforts unsuccessful? What was the significance of the Augsburg Confession?

It is very tempting for us, with the benefit of hindsight, to slip into the trap of assuming that the establishment of a totally separate Lutheran Church was inevitable. To most people in the 1520s this was a horrifying prospect. They could not conceive of there being a permanent division of Christendom. It was bad enough that there was a temporary schism, but to suggest that it might become lasting was to cast doubt on the possibility of restoring public harmony. And without that there would be unending civil conflict which was likely to lead to anarchy and the destruction of 'civilised' living. To the vast majority of Germans who occupied positions of social or political responsibility at the time, it was not a matter of 'if' there would be reconciliation between the Church and the evangelical reformers. It was purely a question of 'when' and 'how'.

The reformers could not predict the 'when', but they were confident about the 'how'. As it was clear that the Pope would not be prepared to make the types of change that were necessary for unity to be restored, it must be left to a Council of the Church, made up of representatives from all areas of Christendom, to pronounce on the important issues. It was generally argued that such a Council must be held in Germany. Many thought that it should be a national Council, with delegates only invited from Germany. These views were acceptable to most Catholics within the Empire, and provided the basis for most of the negotiations that took place between the two groups during the period of Charles's absence from Germany between 1522 and 1529. Only once, at the Diet of Speyer in 1529, did the Catholics attempt to secure the implementation of the terms of the Edict of Worms (see page 36). This led to the representatives of the reformed states making a collective protest against the abandonment of the agreement that no enforcement would take place until after a Council had met. The protesters became known as Protestants, a name that has been applied ever since to all Christian groups having their origins in a breakaway from the Catholic Church.

When Charles turned his attention to the affairs of Germany once again in 1530, it was with the main objective of gaining the maximum possible support, in terms of both men and money, for a war against the Turks. In the previous year the Turks had laid siege to Vienna and had seemed about to pour into the southern provinces of the Empire. There were therefore pressing reasons why he wanted to resolve issues that were divisive. He felt the time was right to present the Muslim Turks with a united Christian front. His efforts to persuade the Pope to summon a Council had been frustrated by delaying tactics from Rome, where it was feared that a Council would attempt to wrest control of the Church's teachings from the Pope. He therefore decided, in effect, to seek to do the work of a Council of the Church at a meeting of the Diet of the Empire. Theologians from both sides were invited to attend the Diet which was to be held at Augsburg.

The Protestants were given the responsibility of attempting to locate the common ground. They were asked to draw up a statement to which they could all agree, and then to negotiate it with the papal representatives. Martin Luther, being under the Imperial ban, was not able to be present. This, in fact, augured well for the success of the venture as he had already come to the conclusion that no accommodation could be reached with the papacy without sacrificing vital elements of his beliefs. But some of his leading supporters disagreed. They still cherished the hope that it would be possible to reform the Church of Rome rather than severing all links with it and establishing a rival organisation. They were led by Philip Melanchthon (1497-1560), who had fallen under Luther's spell at Wittenberg when he was appointed Professor of Greek there at the age of 21. He was a brilliant scholar and was regarded as having one of the best minds of the up-and-coming generation. But he was 14 years younger than Luther, and was in many ways a disciple rather than a colleague. For a long time historians tended to see him only in this light. In recent decades, however, an effort has been made to stress the importance of his contribution to the development of Lutheranism. It can now be seen that he was largely responsible for drawing together Luther's flood of loosely connected ideas and turning them into a coherent set of beliefs. And in doing this he did not merely act as a co-ordinator: he added in much of his own thinking. Melanchthon showed this independence of mind at Augsburg where, in Luther's absence, he was prepared to omit many of his leader's most cherished beliefs, including the priesthood of all believers, from the Protestants' statement in an effort to make it acceptable to the Catholics. But the effort was to no avail. Luther had been right. The papal representatives were willing to accept compromises from the Protestants but they were not prepared to make any of their own. It eventually became clear that an acceptable agreement could not be reached, and all the Protestant members of the Diet withdrew.

The breach had not been healed but there had been real gains for the reformers. At last, after several years of trying and failing, a document had been produced that could act as the theological cement for the Protestant cause, although of course, not for the Anabaptists. This statement of belief, known as the Augsburg Confession, was clearly the result of many compromises and was purposely very inexact in places. But it did provide a basis for Protestant unity that had appeared to be so conspicuously lacking only a year previously at the Marburg Colloquy (see page 68). It is regarded as being Melanchthon's finest work, in which he managed to find the words to bridge an almost unbridgeable gap:

1   One holy Church will abide for ever. For the Church is the congregation of the saints, in which the gospel is rightly taught and the sacraments are rightly administered. For the true unity of the Church it suffices to agree together concerning the teaching of the Gospel and the administration of
5   the Sacraments; it is not necessary that everywhere should exist similar traditions of men, or similar rites and ceremonies instituted by men …The body and blood of Christ are really present and are distributed in the Lord's Supper to those who eat; our churches reject those who teach otherwise … None may publicly teach in church or administer the
10   Sacraments who is not duly called. … Such are the main heads of our teaching, and in it nothing can be found differing from scripture, or from the Catholic Church, or from the Church of Rome as we understand

it from its writers. We are not heretics. Our trouble is with certain abuses that have crept into the Churches without any clear authority. ...
15 The ancient rites are to a large extent carefully preserved among us.

The failure to find sufficient common ground to support an agreement left Charles in a position where it was difficult for him to do anything other than come out firmly on the side of the Catholics and demand that the Edict of Worms be put into effect. But, although he remained in Germany until 1533, his attention was very much directed towards the Turks, and no attempt was made to enforce his authority over the Protestants. He still pinned his hopes on a future Church Council despite the fact that it became increasingly obvious that the reformers had abandoned their attempt at reconciliation. Certainly they were no longer prepared to consider attending a Church Council if it were to be called by the Pope and to be held under his auspices. Yet this was exactly what Charles was trying to arrange.

4 Lutheranism on the Offensive

> **KEY ISSUES** What did Protestant rulers in Germany do in the early 1530s in an attempt to strengthen their position? Why were they successful?

While there had been a realistic hope of reaching an understanding with the Catholic Church, many of the more moderate reformers had been reluctant to do anything that might aggravate the situation. But once the Diets of Speyer and Augsburg had shown in 1529–30 that agreement would only be reached if the Lutherans capitulated totally to the demands of the papacy, the more adventurous leaders of the Protestants were able to exert considerable influence over the movement. By far the most powerful of these was Philip of Hesse. He revelled in the political intrigue and trickery that characterised dealings between states which followed an 'active' external policy.

There had been minor successes in the 1520s in persuading numbers of reforming states to sign defensive alliances with one another in case they were attacked because of their commitment to Protestantism, but the leaders of most of the states which had declared for Luther considered that alliances of this type were provocative. There was even a widespread feeling that, should the Emperor attempt to enforce the Edict of Worms by military might, he should not be resisted, as to do so would be to challenge the teachings of the Bible. The atmosphere changed dramatically after the Diet of Augsburg. It was almost as if the recognition that the split with Rome was permanent had released a flood of Protestant energy and determination. At Philip of Hesse's instigation, an alliance of most of the important Protestant states was formed in 1531. It was known as the League of Schmalkalden, after the town in which the agreement was reached. Although the League was presented as being merely an arrangement for mutual defence, it did in fact operate from the outset as a unified and active pursuer of Protestant interests. It was remarkably successful in its early years when it seemed as if a new power had emerged in international relations.

Charles V, desperate for assistance in 1532 to resist what appeared to be a major offensive by the Turks towards Vienna, was even prepared to agree to suspend all action against members of the League in return for men and money. This agreement, the Religious Truce of Nuremberg, persuaded some of the more timorous Protestant states to join the League. But the real triumph was to come in 1534. The large Dukedom of Württemberg (see the map on page 24) had been administered by the Habsburgs since 1520 when the Duke, Ulrich, had been deposed for breaking Imperial law. He had murdered one of his subjects so that he could woo the newly created widow. He was also by chance a convinced Lutheran. He took his religion very seriously, despite the fact that he was capable of acts of considerable barbarity. Philip of Hesse saw that the restoration of Ulrich would be a great boost to Protestant morale. He planned operations so as to maximise the propaganda gain. There were no negotiations with the Emperor, and no attempt to work within the law. Instead, an agreement was made with Charles's arch-enemy, Francis I of France, for enough money to be supplied to allow Philip to put into the field an army that was larger and better equipped than any other in the region at the time. This army then marched into Württemberg and restored Ulrich virtually unopposed. Lutheranism became the only religion allowed in the dukedom. The blow to Habsburg and Catholic prestige was enormous, especially as Charles accepted the situation and made no attempt to reverse it. It seemed as if the march of Protestantism was irresistible, and that it would only be a matter of time before Catholicism would disappear in Germany. On the deaths of their rulers in 1535 and 1539, Brandenburg and ducal Saxony became Protestant, although Brandenburg did not become Lutheran, preferring instead a type of moderate reform not unlike that introduced by Henry VIII of England. The balance of power was now clearly in the Protestants' favour, especially while the remaining Catholic princes were more afraid of a possible increase in Imperial power than they were of reformed religion, and while Charles V believed that the schism could be healed by persuasion.

5 Charles V on the Offensive

> **KEY ISSUES** Why was Charles V able to defeat the Protestants in Germany? Why did his military success lead to no permanent solution of the religious problem?

Yet the Protestants were in a vulnerable position should Charles decide that the use of force provided the best way forward, and should he be able to devote his whole attention to the issue. They were by no means united, any more than were the Catholics. There was still a marked reluctance on the part of many Protestant princes to engage in war against the Emperor, despite Luther's recent pronouncement that it was morally right to resist God's appointed ruler provided it was in defence of the Gospel. So some states remained outside the League of Schmalkalden, and most of those who were members were likely to put self-interest before the good of the group. It would therefore not be difficult for a skilful manipulator to prize apart the fragile alliance.

Difficulties really began for the reformers in 1541 when what turned out to be Charles V's last attempt to secure the agreement of the Catholics and the Protestants to a common form of words on their fundamental beliefs ended in failure at the Diet of Regensburg. Charles at last admitted to himself that there was no realistic alternative to coercing the Lutherans back to orthodoxy by means of military force. His position was strengthened by the Catholic princes who now saw a possible extension of Imperial power as a lesser evil than the continued expansion of Protestantism which they had previously expected to die away naturally. They were now prepared to support any action Charles might take. At the same time, the credibility of the leading Lutheran prince, Philip of Hesse, had been destroyed by the scandal of his bigamy (see page 58), and he was very much at the Emperor's mercy. So the Protestants were virtually leaderless. All that was needed for the revival of Catholic fortunes in Germany was for Charles to be free from other distractions. And it even seemed that such was the case. A ten-year truce had been signed with the French in 1538, the flood of Ottoman expansion had seemingly been stemmed in Hungary, and difficulties in the Netherlands had been dealt with. The Protestants were rightly very apprehensive. But chance events saved them for the moment. Due to circumstances completely outside Charles's control, war re-opened with France in 1542 and the arrangements in Hungary collapsed. Dealing with the religious schism in Germany once again became a low priority for the Emperor.

Charles was fortunate. France was defeated in 1544 and, in return for lenient terms, agreed not to offer the German Protestants any assistance. In addition, the Turkish threat in Hungary failed to materialise. By 1546 he was at last free to devote all his attention to Germany, secure in the knowledge that he was unlikely to be faced with crises elsewhere in the immediate future. He displayed considerable political skill in handling the situation. He made it clear that he intended no general attack on Protestant states, and that he only sought to punish those - the members of the Schmalkaldic League - who had flouted his rightful authority. He thereby ensured that the cautious reformed states remained inactive. He also managed to enlist the positive support of one of the leading Lutheran princes, Duke Maurice of Saxony, with the promise of the lands and title of the Elector of Saxony. He even contrived to lure the Schmalkaldeners into attacking him, thus removing any doubt that he would generally be seen as being in the right. The outcome of the struggle was not a foregone conclusion. What tipped the balance was the invasion of Electoral Saxony by Duke Maurice. This caused confusion and did much to destroy the morale of the Schmalkaldeners, who had not expected to be attacked from this quarter. Total defeat for the League came in the Battle of Mühlberg in 1547. Its leaders were captured and Charles was free to dictate whatever terms he felt were likely to remain in force once he was no longer personally present in the area. He had learnt as a young man the folly of following a major military success with harsh peace terms that leave the defeated party with little alternative but to re-open hostilities in order to attempt to secure less damaging conditions.

So there were no executions, no seizing of territory by the Habsburgs, and no levying of fines. Instead, a Diet was called to meet in Augsburg (September 1547-May 1548) at which Charles attempted without success to persuade the three estates of the Empire - the electors, the princes and the city authorities - to accept plans for a great strengthening of central government which would have turned Germany into something approaching a nation state. There was also an attempt to impose a religious settlement on the whole Empire in the form of the Augsburg Interim, a document based on Catholic doctrine, with a few insignificant modifications designed to give the appearance of compromise with the Lutherans. All princes and city authorities were instructed to organise religion within their territories in accordance with the Interim, until such time as a Church Council should rule on matters of doctrine. The Interim was almost totally ignored. In practice Charles's victory had achieved nothing beyond showing everybody what were his two priorities in the ruling of the Empire - to secure an increase in his own power at the expense of that of the territorial rulers, and to stamp out Protestantism. But he had completely misjudged what was possible. He seems to have believed that he could order the territorial rulers to return to Catholic practices, that they could do likewise with their subjects, and that then it would happen. He was not aware that tens of thousands of people at all levels of society would have rather died than carry out the terms of the Augsburg Interim.

Historians have criticised Charles for squandering the one opportunity he had to impose his will on the religious life of Germany. They contrast his failure in Germany with the success he achieved in Spain, Italy, Austria and the Netherlands. But this judgement is somewhat unfair. While it is true that he made mistakes in Germany from 1548 onwards, so that by 1555 his position was weaker than it had been before the successful campaign of 1546-7, it must be remembered that he had set himself virtually unobtainable goals. His mistake was more in setting himself unrealistic targets rather than in failing to achieve them. By the 1540s it was too late for Lutheranism to be destroyed as an organised religion in most of northern and eastern Germany.

6 The Peace of Augsburg

KEY ISSUE What was the significance of the Peace of Augsburg?

The impossibility of the aim was finally recognised in 1555, when at another Diet of Augsburg an agreement was drawn up in which it was assumed that the schism was permanent, and in which arrangements were made for its management. It was probably appropriate that Charles was not present at the Diet. He left the arrangements to be made by his brother, Frederick, who was soon to take over from him as Emperor, while he journeyed to the Netherlands to prepare for the handing over of his other responsibilities to his son, the future Philip II of Spain. The terms of the so-called Peace of Augsburg were to remain in force well into the next century, and although their endurance could not have been foretold at the time, they were a clear recognition of the political and religious realities of Germany.

1   His Imperial Majesty and we, the electors, princes, and estates of the Holy Empire will not make war upon any estate of the empire on account of the Augsburg Confession and the doctrine, religion, and faith of the same, nor injure nor do violence to those estates that hold it ...
5   On the other hand, the estates that have accepted the Augsburg Confession shall suffer [those] adhering to the old religion, to abide in like manner by their religion, faith, church usages, ordinances, and ceremonies ...
    But all others who are not adherents of either of the above-
10 mentioned religions are not included in this peace, but shall be altogether excluded ...
    But when [those] adhering to the old religion or to the Augsburg Confession, wish, for the sake of their religion, to go to another place and settle there, such going and coming, and the sale of property and
15 goods shall be everywhere unhindered, permitted and granted ...

In each state there was to be one religion - either Catholicism or Lutheranism. The government of the state was to make the decision. No state was to attempt to force its views on any other state. People were to be free to move, with their belongings, to a state where their religion was practised. This arrangement has been almost universally praised as an example of enlightened good sense and tolerance. This it certainly was, but it was also an indicator that the early fire had gone from the Reformation. Luther had been dead for nearly a decade and those of the first generation of reformers who remained alive were old and tired. On the other side, Charles V, who for 30 years had been the driving force behind the efforts to end the schism, had reached the point where he recognised that his energies were largely spent. The Peace of Augsburg marked a half-way stage in the Reformation. The early contest had been declared a draw when peace and rest had appeared preferable to continuing struggle and insecurity. But the battle was far from over: Calvin and his supporters, and the Popes of the Counter-Reformation and their supporters were soon to rekindle the fires of sectarian strife.

Working on Chapter 6

You need to make notes on the sequence of political events between 1521 and 1555 so that they will be available to revise from later on. Make sure that each of the events in the Key Dates list is included in what you write. However, the most important part of your work on this chapter is reaching conclusions on *why* things happened as they did. A good first step in doing this is to think through answers to the questions included in the issues boxes. When you have done this you should be in a good position to write an answer to the question, 'Why did Charles V fail to prevent the establishment and spread of Lutheranism, and why did he fail to destroy it?'.

Answering structured and essay questions on Chapter 6

It is possible that in one part of a structured question you will be asked to give a straightforward narrative account of the main events affecting the spread and survival of Lutheranism in Germany. You should therefore ensure that you commit to memory the important facts included in the chapter. However, it is most likely that you will also be required to provide an explanation of the reasons for Lutheranism's spread and survival. Plan an answer to the following questions:

a) What actions did Lutherans in Germany take during the 1530s to protect themselves?

b) Why were the Lutherans able to resist the attempts of Charles V to destroy them?

The essay questions you will be expected to answer on this topic will typically be variations on '*Why did Lutheranism become so firmly established in Germany?*' You may be lucky enough to be given the question in its straightforward form, in which case you will need to think of a number of points beginning with the word 'because'. But more probably you will encounter one of the variations, in which a possible answer is given and you are asked to comment. These variations are effectively, of course, 'challenging statement' questions.

Summary Diagram
The Politics of Lutheranism

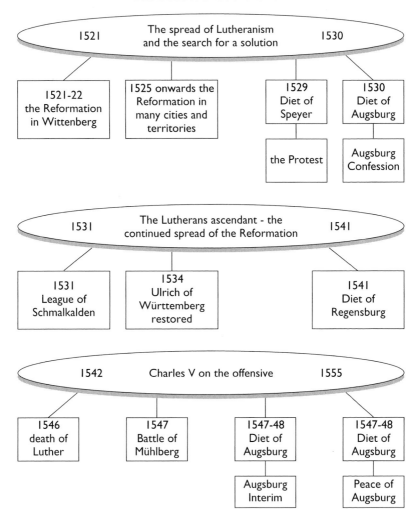

Some examples of 'challenging statement' questions are:

'It was the printing press that ensured the spread and success of Lutheranism in Germany.' Discuss.

'The success of the German Reformation was largely due to the political difficulties of Charles V.' Do you agree?

'The religion of the German Princes.' How far does this explain the success of Lutheranism?

Make a list of the factors that led to the success of Lutheranism. Test out a variety of ways of grouping these factors into sets. You could, for instance, form two sets - 'the strengths of the reformers' and 'the weaknesses of their opponents', or a number of sets based on 'economic', 'social', 'political', etc. Find as many possible ways of grouping as you can. Which ones are most effective for you in explaining what happened? One that often works well is to divide the factors into two sets: a group of 'personal factors' (things done and not done by named individuals, especially Martin Luther and Charles V), and a group of 'impersonal factors' (aspects of the situation that were outside any one person's control). This is particularly helpful in drawing attention to the large part played by Luther in the German Reformation, but it also serves to remind us that he was by no means all-important. Once you have decided on the grouping that best suits you, you will have done the thinking necessary to ensure that you can discuss general questions on the Reformation in Germany with insight.

Source-based questions on Chapter 6

1. The Augsburg Confession, 1530
Read the extracts from the Augsburg Confession on pages 93-4, and answer the following questions:

a) What evidence do the extracts contain to suggest that the document was written by a Protestant? *(3 marks)*

b) What were the motives of the author? Support your answer with evidence. *(3 marks)*

c) What evidence does the document contain to suggest that it was written by a Lutheran rather than by a Zwinglian? *(3 marks)*

d) What are the implications of the final sentence (line 15)? *(3 marks)*

e) From your own knowledge, explain why was Luther unhappy about the wording of the Augsburg Confession? *(3 marks)*

2. The Peace of Augsburg, 1555
Read the extracts from the Peace of Augsburg on page 98, and answer the following questions:

a) Would it be correct to claim that the Peace of Augsburg was intended to prohibit religious persecution within the Empire? Explain your answer. *(5 marks)*

b) What are the assumptions lying behind the fourth extract (lines 12-15)? What do these assumptions suggest were the attitudes at the time towards civil liberties? *(5 marks)*

c) Could the terms of the Peace be considered to be a victory for either Charles V or the Protestants? Explain your answer. *(5 marks)*

Further Reading

There are hundreds of books in English that deal with the Reformation in Germany. As you will not have an endless amount of time to spend on this topic, you must be very selective about what you choose to read. Do not be tempted to spend time on a book merely because it is relevant and available.

If your study of this topic is going to be extensive, it makes sense to begin with a recent major work on the subject. Particularly appropriate would be R. Marius, *Martin Luther: the Christian between God and death* (Harvard University Press, 1999).

Although this is more detailed than you are likely to require, it would be worth looking at to gain an overview of the current state of research on Luther. Reading the Preface would provide you with some helpful insights. You could also use the index to track down information on specific events or issues.

If, however, you can only spare time to look at one book, you should read at least part of R.H. Bainton, *Here I Stand* (Hodder and Stoughton).

Although this was first published, in America, in 1950, it is still the most readable and stimulating biography of Martin Luther. It is particularly good on Luther the man, and on his theology. Reading it is likely to make you want to know more!

The same effect is likely to be created by G.R. Elton, *Reformation Europe, 1517–1559* (Fontana, 1963).

This is just the type of book, in paperback, that it is worth buying. It will repay reading over and over again. Each time you will find something new to interest you. Elton's interpretations are usually challenging and controversial. The more you know, the more you will gain from it. The book covers the major themes of European political history in this period: it is not restricted to the Reformation.

The most readable and reliable book which looks at the thinking and teaching of a range of leading Reformation figures from Luther to Calvin (although it is quite difficult in places), is B.M.G. Reardon, *Religious Thought in the Reformation* (Longman, 1981).

To read even one chapter of it is worthwhile. You will gain a variety of insights, including into your own ability to handle philosophical and theological ideas.

Any of the writings of A.G. Dickens are worth looking at. The easiest to read is a biography of Luther which was originally aimed at the A-level and undergraduate market. If you read it, try to spot Dickens's interpretation of Luther's motives. The book is A.G. Dickens, *Martin Luther and the Reformation* (E.U.P., 1967).

Equally worth dipping into are the works of G.R. Potter on Ulrich Zwingli. If possible try to read a chapter or two of G.R. Potter, *Zwingli* (C.U.P., 1976), which is now the standard biography. It is generally very readable (less so on Zwingli's teachings) and offers many insights into how the Reformation actually happened.

An absolute 'must' for students who aspire to the highest grade at A-level (and for teachers) is Scribner's brief discussion of recent research findings on the subject. It is very difficult, but is well worth struggling with. It is: R.W. Scribner, *The German Reformation* (Macmillan, 1986).

Sources on Luther and the German Reformation, 1517-55

There is no shortage of published primary sources on the Reformation in Germany. Luckily, some of it is readily available and cheap.

Two collections of documentary extracts, in paperback, should be in every school and college library. These are:

1. E.G. Rupp and B. Drewery, *Martin Luther* (Edward Arnold, 1970) and
2. G.R. Potter, *Huidrych Zwingli* (Edward Arnold, 1978).

A full documentary account of the proceedings at the Diet of Worms, using reports that are both hostile to and supportive of Luther, are to be found in:

3. James Atkinson, *The Trial of Luther* (Batsford, 1971).

A rich source of illustrations on the subject is:

4. R.H. Bainton, *Here I Stand* (Hodder and Stoughton, 1950).

Index